蚌埠市博物馆
铜镜集萃

蚌埠市博物馆　编著

文物出版社

目　录　Contents

概 述 PREFACE

一

蚌埠市位于安徽省中北部,地理位置东经117°11′~117°31′,北纬32°49′~33°01′。境北与濉溪县、宿州市、灵璧县、泗县接壤,境南与淮南市、凤阳县相连,境东与明光市和江苏省泗洪县毗邻,境西与蒙城县、凤台县搭界。津浦铁路纵贯城市南北,淮河自西向东穿城而过。蚌埠市辖怀远、固镇、五河三县和淮上、龙子湖、蚌山、禹会四区。总面积为5952平方公里,总人口约为358.31万。

古代,淮河出怀远荆山口至蚌埠地域,水流趋缓,水质清澈,水草茂密,盛产河蚌与珍珠。《尚书·禹贡》中记载:"泗滨浮磬,淮夷蠙珠暨鱼。"清《凤阳府志》记载:"蚌步集在灵璧西南160里,乃古采珠之地。"因此,蚌埠又称"珠城"。

蚌埠地区历史悠久,自古以来就是人类生产生活的重要地区之一。考古资料表明,在距今约三万年前,蚌埠地区已有人类活动踪迹;七千年前双墩文化已经显露出文明曙光;四千年前此处曾是涂山氏国所在地,《左传·哀公七年》载"禹合诸侯于涂山",即指涂山禹会村遗址。

夏商周时期这里曾是淮夷族聚居区。至春秋时期,蚌埠地区属钟离国。战国时期,蚌埠地区曾分别为徐、鲁、宋、吴、越、楚等国邑地。秦王朝建立后,实行郡县制,蚌埠地域属九江郡、泗水郡所辖。汉代蚌埠地区淮河以北归属沛郡,淮河以南归属淮南国,后淮南国改为九江郡。三国时期蚌埠属魏地,淮河以北归属谯郡,淮河以南隶属淮南国。此后两晋南北朝时期战乱不止,蚌埠地域建制更迭频繁。隋唐时期至唐开元二十一年(733年)后,蚌埠淮河以南属淮南道监察,淮河以北属河南道监察。五代十国政权更迭建制纷乱,直至后周显德五年(958年)夺取蚌埠整个地区,淮河以北由徐州辖,淮河以南由濠州辖。北宋时(960~1127年)蚌埠淮河以北隶属

于新置灵璧县,为淮南东路宿州所辖,淮河以南只存钟离县,为淮南西路濠州所辖。南宋时期,至南宋宝祐五年(1257年),蚌埠西部重置荆山县。为淮南西路怀远军所辖。咸淳七年(1271年),蚌埠东北置五河县,为淮南东路淮南军所辖。南宋、金对峙时期,今固镇县先为宿州蕲县、灵璧县及泗州虹县分领,后为宿州、灵璧、荆山、五河等县分领。元朝时期,元至元二十八年(1291年)撤销怀远军,改荆山县为怀远县属濠州,蚌埠市区西属怀远县,东属钟离县;固镇县为宿州及灵璧、五河、怀远县分领,五河县属泗州。明朝时期,洪武年间,钟离县先后改为中立县、临淮县,增设凤阳县;蚌埠市区西属怀远县,东属凤阳县;固镇县分属宿州及怀远、灵璧、五河、凤阳县。濠州先更名临濠府后更名凤阳府,全境均属凤阳府。清朝时期,清沿袭明制全境属凤阳府,雍正年间泗州脱离凤阳府,五河县属泗州,其余均属凤阳府。其中凤阳县主簿衙门驻蚌埠,清同治二年(1863年),划凤阳县马村沟以西、怀远县席家沟以东、灵璧县后楼为蚌埠独立行政区,置三县司,直属安徽省凤阳府。1947年1月1日,蚌埠正式设市,直属安徽省,为安徽省第一个省辖市。

二

铜镜是古代照面饰容的日常生活用具。古代铜镜,正面光滑可鉴,用于照容;反面则多修饰图案花纹。它铸制精良、形态美观、图纹华丽、铭文丰富,因此古代铜镜既是古人生活的实用器,又是精美的工艺品,是我国古代文化遗产中的珍品。

关于铜镜的起源和演变,著名学者梁上椿曾在《古镜研究总论》中指出:"止水—鉴盆中静水—无水光鉴—光面铜片—铜片背而加钮—素背镜—素地加绘彩—改绘彩加铸图文—加铸字铭"。由此可见,铜镜的由来是人们由止水能照

容演变而来。我国铜镜历史悠久，根据目前的考古资料证实，我国铜镜历史最早可以追溯到四千多年前的齐家文化。20世纪70年代，齐家文化出土的两面圆形、背部置钮并装饰花纹的铜镜，开创了我国"圆板具钮"镜的先河，对以后铜镜的发展产生了极大影响。

商周时期，是我国青铜工艺发展的鼎盛时期，但出土的铜镜却寥寥二十余面，并且多集中于黄河上游地区，与其他青铜器的璀璨相比，商周铜镜尚未形成完整的体系，处于萌芽阶段。

春秋战国时期，是铜镜发展的流行期。这一时期铜镜迅速发展，成就斐然。铸制轻巧，纹饰精致，线条流畅，一扫前一阶段铜镜幼稚拙朴的风格，代表了铜镜工艺的新风格。汉代是我国铜镜发展的鼎盛时期，《古镜图录》曾载，"刻画之精巧，文字之瑰奇，辞旨之温雅，一器而三善备焉者莫镜若也"，恰如其分的概括了两汉铜镜的特点。三国两晋南北朝是铜镜发展的中衰期。经过一段时间的低迷，到隋唐时期，铜镜又迎来了发展的繁荣期，唐代铜镜如同这个开放的时代一样，既改变了战国镜的轻巧，也摆脱了汉镜的拘谨，无论在造型还是题材方面比前代都有所突破，这一时期铜镜种类繁多，样式新颖，新工艺、新造型、新纹饰不断涌现。五代、宋、金、元以后，铜镜逐渐衰落。至明清时期，铜镜慢慢退出了历史舞台，逐渐被玻璃镜所取代。

从形式上看，目前考古出土的铜镜，尽管有方镜、花式镜、有柄镜等，但圆板具钮镜一直是中国铜镜的最主要形式。从常用的主题装饰图案上看，尽管历代各具特色，但珍禽奇兽始终是一个重要题材。从战国时代婉转曲折的蟠螭、蟠虺，直到明清时代腾云驾雾的云龙，作为中华民族图腾的"龙"的形象未曾在铜镜上绝迹。今天，铜镜虽然退出了历史舞台，但它们的神韵却不因时间的流逝而泯灭，将在中华文明的艺术宝库中熠熠生辉。

三

春秋战国时期在中国古代铜镜发展史中是一个成熟和大发展的时期，是中国古代铜镜由稚朴走向成熟的过渡阶段，也是铜镜的铸造中心由北开始向南迁移的重要时期。春秋战国时期铜镜在夏、商、周三代的基础上，有了突飞猛进的全面发展，无论是铸造工艺，还是铸造数量，都大大超过了以前。

"山"字纹镜，是战国时期较为流行的一种铜镜，一般按所饰"山"字的数量分三山、四山、五山和六山镜四种。其中又以四山镜居多。1973年蚌埠市西郊八里桥墓葬出土的四山镜，是本地区目前发现时代最早的铜镜。该镜为圆形，四弦钮，方钮座。镜背纹饰由地纹和主纹组合而成。地纹为羽状纹，地纹之上，由中心处向外延伸出四组连贯的花瓣，每组两瓣，在各组花瓣的顶端又连接一棒槌状的长叶纹，长叶纹均逆时针方向排列。四组花瓣和长叶纹将镜背分四区，每区置一左旋"山"字，"山"字笔画较瘦长。在各"山"字的右胁，装饰一片花瓣，全镜花瓣均以窄带纹相连接，共十二花瓣四长叶。素宽卷缘。

汉代是我国统一多民族封建国家的强盛时期，封建经济呈现了空前的繁荣。随着封建经济的发展，手工业生产的规模和水平都有了很大的发展和提高，金属铸造工艺不断进步。铜镜是汉代铜铸造品中最多的产品，不仅在数量上比战国时期多，而且在制作形式和艺术表现手法上也有了很大发展。在本馆藏镜中，汉镜数量最多，约占馆藏铜镜的30%。本书辑录汉镜43面，纹饰包括连弧纹、铭文圈带、博局纹、四乳或者多乳禽兽花鸟纹、神兽画像纹、龙虎纹等。

连弧纹铭文镜是汉镜中出土数量多、流行范围广的镜类之一，流行于西汉中期至东汉早期，其特征是钮座外内区纹饰为连弧纹，外区为铭文带，共同构成主题纹饰。根据铭文内容，分为日光镜和昭明镜等，本书辑录的日光镜2面，昭明镜9面，日有憙铭连弧纹镜1面。两面日光镜直径都在7厘米左右，镜体较薄，制作较为粗糙，铭文内容均为"见日之光，天下大明"。本馆所藏昭明镜较日光镜形制要大一些，镜体厚重，制作规整，形制一般是圆形，圆钮，圆钮座。座外围一周内向八连弧纹，其外两周栉齿纹之间有铭文圈带。昭明镜完整铭文应为"内清质以昭明，光辉象夫兮日月，心忽扬而愿忠，然雍塞而不泄"，不过由于镜子大小不一，因此常有省字、减字的现象出现，但总的来说，省字还是在一定的规范之内。还有一种情况在每字之间夹一"而"字，这些"而"是为了补足布字不足的空缺，没有实际的文字含义。1983年怀远县龙亢向桥公社花砖墓出土的一面日有憙铭连弧纹镜，直径15.1厘米，圆形，圆钮，柿蒂纹钮座。座外饰一周凸弦纹及内向八连弧纹，间饰短线条组成的简单的纹饰。其外两周栉齿纹之间有铭文圈带："日有憙，月有富，乐毋事，宜酒食，居必安，毋患忧，竽瑟侍，心志欢，乐已茂，固常。"此类的镜子，尺寸比日光镜和昭明镜要大，一般都在14厘米以上，根据考古发掘资料来看，这类镜子流行年代要稍晚。

博局镜，又称规矩镜，因镜纹以规则的"T、L、V"形装饰，外国学者也称之为"T、L、V"镜。现在普遍认为，博局纹起源于汉代的六博戏棋局。博戏是古代的一种赌输赢、角胜负的游戏，带有赌博色彩。秦汉时，社会上广泛流行，上至王公，下至百姓均乐此不疲。其制作程式相当统一，一般为圆钮，圆钮座或柿蒂纹钮座，座外围双线凹面方框，方框内有纹饰或铭文。内区四组"T、L、V"博局纹将其分为四方八区，填饰四神、羽人、鸟兽或几何纹。内外区之间多加饰铭文带。宽缘，缘上饰双线波折纹、锯齿纹或者云气纹。最早的博局纹见于西汉武帝时期，但博局纹主要流行于西汉晚期至东汉早期。王莽时期博局镜尤盛，纹饰细腻，制作精良，水平极高。

到东汉中晚期，博局纹及其相间的纹饰趋向简化，制作粗糙，日趋没落。到魏晋南北朝初期，博局纹逐渐消失匿迹了。博局纹是汉镜纹饰中流行时间最长的一种，也是汉镜中最为优秀的一种。

本书辑录博局纹类镜15面。2009年蚌埠市禹会区九龙集万隆汽配场墓葬群，出土的一面东汉博局镜，直径17.8厘米，边厚0.5厘米，重798克。该镜为圆形，圆钮，柿蒂纹钮座。座外饰凸弦纹方框和双线凹面方框各一周。其间十二枚圆座乳钉和十二地支铭文绕钮相间环列。凹面方框外环列八枚圆座乳钉纹和四组"T、L、V"形博局纹，乳钉纹和博局纹将镜背分成四方八区，空白处填饰青龙、白虎、朱雀、玄武四神，各据一方，每神配一只禽兽作装饰，隔"V"纹相对而立。其外一周铭文圈带："尚方作竟真大巧，上有仙人不知老，渴饮玉泉饥食枣，浮游天下敖四海。"这是一面典型的"尚方"铭四神博局镜，造型规整，纹饰细腻。"尚方"是汉代为皇室制作御用物品的官署，属少府。尚方铭镜为御制镜，质量上乘，纹饰精美。当时，民间有很多工匠假借尚方制镜的名义作镜，相比而言，质量粗糙。

四乳禽兽纹类镜，其主要特征是钮座外四乳间环绕着虺、飞禽、兽、四神等纹饰。根据四乳间环绕的不同纹饰，将其分成四乳四虺镜、四乳禽兽纹镜、四乳四神镜。本书辑录四乳四虺镜4面，四乳禽兽纹类镜4面。1990年天河乡供销社汉墓出土的一面四乳四虺镜，形制为圆形，圆钮，圆钮座。座外围一周凸弦纹。钮座与凸弦纹之间有短线组成的简单纹饰。其外两周栉齿纹之间，等距离的分布着四枚圆座乳钉纹，空白处填以四虺，四虺成钩形躯体，两端同形，虺的身躯两侧各填饰一只禽鸟纹。素宽平缘。虺，是古代传说中著名的山林鬼物，被认为是图案稍简化的龙的形象。《述异记》载："虺五百年化为蛟，蛟千年化为龙。"

神兽画像纹类镜，分为神兽镜和画像镜两种，主要流行于东汉中晚期至魏晋南北朝时期的长江流域。皆是以浮雕手法表现主题纹饰神像、龙虎等题材的镜类，纹饰题材主要取自于神话故事和民间传说，寓意深刻，构思巧妙。本书辑录神兽画像纹类镜2面，其中画像镜1面，神兽镜1面。画像镜主纹饰多为东王公、西王母端坐，旁有侍者，配有车马、禽兽、羽人等，均为圆形，圆钮，内外区间多有铭文圈带，镜缘部饰云纹、鸟兽纹、锯齿纹和波折纹等。神兽画像纹类镜是东汉时代新兴的镜类，其纹饰、形制和浮雕技法，标志着中国铜镜发展到了一个新阶段。

龙虎纹类镜，分为龙纹、虎纹和龙虎纹三类，主要流行于东汉中晚期，一直延续到魏晋南北朝时期。本书辑录龙虎纹镜2面，均为龙虎对峙镜，圆形，大圆钮，钮外高浮雕一龙一虎夹钮对峙。虎纹镜5面，均为三虎镜。1994年怀远县出土的一面三虎镜，直径11厘米，边厚1.5厘米，重364克。该镜为圆形，圆钮，圆钮座。座外高浮雕式三虎绕钮，其中两虎对峙，一虎跟随，身躯重点部位饰大乳钉加以突出，三虎皆作蹬踏状。外饰铭文圈带"龙氏作竟四夷（服），多贺君家人民息，胡羌殄（灭）天下复，□时节"。外饰一周栉齿纹。宽缘，缘上饰锯齿纹和双线波折纹。

魏晋南北朝是中国历史上政权更迭最频繁的时期。由于长期的封建割据和连绵不断的战争，使这一时期经济、文化的发展受到特别的影响。铜镜制造业也受到了一定程度的打击，出现了短暂的中衰期。本书收录此时期的铜镜2面。其中一面位至三公铭龙凤纹镜，直径11厘米，边厚0.27厘米，重160克。圆形，圆钮，圆钮座。钮座上下两条竖线间各饰"位至"和"三公"铭文，钮左侧饰一只"S"形曲体凤鸟，右侧饰一条"S"曲体龙。外围一周栉齿纹。素宽缘。有些学者认为，这类镜子是从东汉时期流行的"双头龙凤镜"衍化而来。

隋朝建立后，结束了三百多年南北分裂的局面，继之而起的唐朝，国家统一，封建政治经济

文化繁荣，手工业也呈现一片兴盛景象，促进了铜镜制作工艺的大幅度提高。唐代铜镜的造型、题材、铸造都别具一格，是中国铜镜高度发展的时期。唐镜如同这个开放的时代一样，既改变了战国镜的轻巧，也打破了汉代铜镜规矩严谨的样式。形制上不再拘泥于圆形，出现了葵花形、菱花形，纹饰上出现了异域元素，题材上摆脱了黄老学说、羽化升仙的影响，更加贴近生活，那充满活力的鸾翔凤舞、花鲜兽跃的图纹正是升平盛世的印记。

本书辑录唐代铜镜22面，以瑞兽禽鸟纹和花卉纹居多，其中瑞兽禽鸟纹镜13面，花卉纹镜8面，形制有圆形、菱花形、葵花形，主题纹饰有瑞兽纹、瑞兽葡萄纹、瑞兽鸾鸟纹、禽鸟纹、双鸾衔绶纹、交枝花鸟纹、折枝花纹、宝相花纹、神仙人物故事纹等。

瑞兽葡萄镜，又称海兽葡萄镜，《金石索》载："海马蒲桃竟，博古图不释其意，或取天马徕自西极及张骞使得蒲桃归之异欤？"由此可见，葡萄镜的纹样源于西域，汉武帝时，张骞出使西域后将葡萄引入中原，史料记载，在当时的上林苑已有葡萄种植。唐代时，葡萄广泛种植，葡萄纹样也开始流行。而瑞兽纹饰在中国自有传统，六朝、隋、初唐铜镜上瑞兽盛行。瑞兽葡萄镜是把当时流行的两种纹样结合起来，创造出唐代独有的新镜类。本书收录瑞兽葡萄镜2面，形制均为圆形。瑞兽葡萄镜把瑞兽和葡萄合在一起，再加上鸟禽花枝相应，呈现出一幅生动活泼的画面：祥云瑞兽，翻腾闹海，葡萄串枝，藤蔓鹊绕，优美轻快，整幅画面几乎没有留下空白，缝隙间也只添了少许的枝叶和藤蔓，配以飞蝶雀鸟穿梭其中，千姿百态，欣欣向荣，富丽堂皇。

本馆所藏的一面雀绕花枝镜，直径10厘米，边厚0.5厘米，重175克，八瓣菱花形，圆钮。钮外四禽鸟四折枝花相间环绕。四禽鸟各两组，一组两鹊振翅飞翔，尾翼伸展；一组两雁双脚站立，羽翼未张。四禽鸟间有形状稍异的两组折枝

花对称分布。边缘展翅的四蜂蝶与四朵两叶一苞的折枝花相间排列。主题纹饰营造出一副安静祥和的画面,是唐代盛世之下,人们热爱生活、享受太平的真实写照。

1975年我市征集的一面折枝花鸟镜,直径21.8厘米,边厚0.5厘米,重1252克,形制为圆形,圆钮,花瓣钮座。座外四花枝绕钮排列,花枝为五叶一苞的折枝花,形态一致,绽蕊怒放,每一花枝下饰一鹊,形态或展翅,或作回首状。四花枝之间饰一两叶一苞的小折枝花。镜面布局错落有致、繁而不乱,禽鸟形态栩栩如生,折枝花尽情绽放,一派欣欣向荣之景。

真子飞霜镜,本书辑录1面,形制为八出葵花形,龟钮,荷叶形钮座。钮左一人峨冠博带,坐而抚琴,前设香案,后依竹林。钮右一凤鸟,振翅翘尾舞于石上,其上有树两株。钮上为云上日月出,钮下为石山水池,水波涟漪,池内伸曲柄荷叶,叶上突出一龟,正好形成镜钮。关于真子飞霜镜所反映的含义,目前尚无定论,一说认为"真子"即"真孝子"的简称,"飞霜"为古琴曲调十二操之一,履霜操的别称,讲述的是在周宣王时期尹伯奇被放逐于野的寓意。

尹伯奇是周宣王的大臣尹吉甫的儿子,他精通音律,也是位出名的孝子。伯奇的生母死后,他的后母想让自己的儿子伯卦承袭爵位和财产,就向尹吉甫诬陷伯奇调戏自己,并让他躲在暗处观看。后母捉来毒蜂藏进衣袖,在伯奇向她请安的时候偷偷将毒蜂放出。伯奇不顾被蜇的危险,用手替后母在衣服上捉毒蜂。尹吉甫离得远没看见毒蜂,认为是伯奇行为不轨,把他赶出了家门。伯奇不愿意申辩,挟着自己心爱的琴,被迫离开了家。

他独自在荒野中,又冻又饿,想到自己所受的冤屈,作出了一首凄惋的琴歌《履霜操》(又称《飞霜操》)。周宣王在巡视的路上,听到了这首《履霜操》,对陪同的尹吉甫说:"这唱歌的一定是个受了很大冤枉的孝子。"尹吉甫听着儿子的歌声,又疑又悔,派人找到了伯奇。事实真相大白,尹吉甫愤怒地杀死了后妻,把伯奇接回了家,父子骨肉又重新团聚在一起。

唐朝灭亡后,中国进入了五代十国、宋、辽、金、元时期。五代十国动乱不断,北宋的建立结束了中原动乱的局面,但北方少数民族辽、西夏、金的崛起,使得北宋和辽、西夏并立,南宋和金对峙,连年的战乱导致铜料匮乏,铜镜铸造业从此一蹶不振,铜镜自此之后进入了衰落期。元朝的大统一,使这时期的历史呈现出十分复杂的局面,各地政治、经济发展不平衡。由于政局的变化和民族传统的不同,这一时期的铜镜也存在着明显的时代差别和民族风格。

本书收录五代时期铜镜3面,1986年蚌埠市淮光乡仇家岗出土的一面刘思训造铭省坊镜,属都省铜坊镜,镜上有铸镜工匠款识的铭文,该镜直径16.1厘米,边厚0.25厘米,重342克,形制为圆形,圆钮。钮外环一周双连珠纹构成的大方框,框内饰连钱纹。两组连珠纹间的空白处,左右两侧各铸有四字铭文"省坊镜面","刘思训造";上下部各填饰四组花卉纹。方框四角填饰四组钱纹,框外满铺龟背纹。两周连珠纹为廓,素宽缘。

宋镜器体轻薄,装饰简洁,注重实用,不崇华侈。形状仍以圆形为主,亦有方形、弧形、菱形以及带柄等多种形式。镜背纹饰风格更趋于写实,图案处理融入绘画风格,以花鸟鱼虫、龙蟠凤逸居多,所描绘的动植物图案,形象准确,姿态生动,构图丰富多变。在冶铸方面,宋镜的合金成分发生了变化,含锡量明显减少,含铅量大增。这带来了铜镜质地、色泽的变化,对后世铜镜有着深远的影响。本书收录宋、金时期铜镜23面,纹饰主要有花卉纹镜、双鱼纹镜、花鸟纹镜、神仙人物故事纹镜、湖州铭文镜等。

缠枝花草镜,主题纹饰为各种不同形式的花枝、花瓣,多用浅细浮雕法处理,弱枝细叶相互盘绕,形成纤巧隽秀的图案。1975年本市征集的一面缠枝四花镜,直径14.8厘米,边厚0.1厘米,重200克。形制为亚字形,桥形小钮,花瓣钮座。座外环绕四朵缠枝花,花头对着亚字形的内角。构图枝叶连亘、互相缠绕,画面细致,描绘逼真,具有强烈的现实感和韵律节奏感。

蚌埠市博物馆所藏的一面双凤镜,直径26厘米,圆形,圆钮。双凤绕钮对飞,形态一致。双凤头顶有矮冠羽,细颈弯曲,双翅伸展,身上羽毛丰满,尾翼细长飘逸。双凤之间填充云气纹。外围一周凸弦纹,窄缘。该镜双凤羽翅刻画细致,形态逼真,极富动感,整个图案线条纤细、精致美观,整个画面给人一种轻松浪漫的感觉,体现出宋代匠师的卓越技艺。

湖州镜,是宋代最流行的镜类,形制有葵花形、亚字形、方形、桃形等。本书收录湖州铭文镜8面,其中葵花形镜5面,亚字形镜1面,桃形镜2面,铭文主要有"湖州真石家念二叔照子","湖州仪枫桥石家,真正一色青铜照子"等。值得注意的是,宋代称镜为"照子",是因为宋人避讳甚严,赵匡胤之祖"敬",因避"镜"讳,改名"照子"或"监子"。绍兴三十二年(1162年)朝廷规定可以不避此讳,绍熙元年(1190年)又重新严格避讳制度,因此这段时间有些铜镜也称"镜"。湖州镜大约源于北宋晚期,盛行于南宋初期到中期,主要流行于南方地区。北宋末年,由于战乱,北方人口大举南迁,经济重心随之南移,手工业也随即发展起来,当时的湖州、饶州、临安府、平安府等地铸镜闻名全国。湖州镜几乎没有纹饰,仅铸有作坊主姓名或价格等,往往在名号上冠以"真"或"真正",以表明正宗,防止假冒。

许由巢父故事镜,直径18厘米,边厚0.8厘米,重1250克,形制为圆形,圆钮,钮顶平。镜背上部是几座巍峨峭拔峰峦,中峰顶端一树枝虬干曲,垂于山腰。镜背下部,山脚下河边一人牵牛,一人坐地,两人作对话姿态。素宽平缘。题材源于古代传说:上古时代,部落联盟的首领选拔实行禅让制。尧在考察他的继位人时,十分注重接班人的群众基础。尧听说阳城(今山西洪洞)的巢父、许由是大贤者,便前去拜访。初见巢父,巢父不受;继访许由,许由也不接受禅让,且遁耕于洪洞的九箕山中。尧执意让位,紧追不舍,再次寻见许由时,恳求许由做九州长。许由觉得王位固且不受,岂有再当九州长之理,顿感蒙受大辱,遂奔至溪边,清洗听脏了的耳朵。

许由在河边洗耳朵时,恰遇隐居树上的好友巢父牵牛前来饮水。巢父得知许由洗耳的原由后,说:"这个都是你自己不好,你果然诚心避世,何不深藏起来呢?现在你的两耳已经污浊了,洗过的水也是污浊的,我这洁净的牛,不来饮你污浊的水。"说完,把牛牵到上游去饮水了……许由巢父故事镜正是取自这一片段。

中国铜镜自唐末、五代起日趋衰落,金代铜镜却在北国异军突起,呈现多样化的风格。金朝是女真人建立的北方政权,反映在铜镜艺术上呈现多元化的文化面貌,以其民族习俗和社会风尚的粗犷厚重融入铜镜艺术。镜面风格与同时期的湖州镜区别很大。金代官府对铜的管理极其严格,有铜禁制度,私人禁止铸造铜镜,因此金代铜镜的边缘往往錾刻官府验记文字和押记。金代铜镜还出现了新形式和新题材,以双鱼镜、人物故事镜为多见。本书辑录金代铜镜9面,纹饰主要有双鱼镜、摩羯镜、花卉镜、人物故事镜等。

摩羯纹带柄镜,桃形,长柄。镜背高浮雕饰一摩羯展翅高飞,翱翔于翻滚的海面。镜背上方祥云中露出一弯新月。素窄凸缘。摩羯(makara),梵语译音,为佛教语,源于印度传说中的河水之精灵,其地位类似中国的河神。摩羯传入中国后,经过中国佛教的重新诠释,形象演变为龙首鱼身,成为佛教中的一种神鱼,是如来佛在水中的化身。

本书收录人物故事镜2面,其中一面吴牛喘月故事镜,形制为圆形,圆钮。钮上中间出置一单线方框。其外天空中烟云映带,一弯新月。水天相

接，翻滚的层层波浪，占据镜背的大部分。钮的左右两侧各有一仙人，手托宝盘。钮下水中一牛，翘首张望，呼呼喘气。素宽平缘。纹饰取材于吴牛喘月的典故：生于江南的水牛，畏热，见月误以为日，故喘。

明清时期制镜较两宋时期也有所发展，镜体更加厚重，工艺也更加精致。大量仿汉式铜镜在这一时期出现，吉祥铭文镜十分流行，主要铭文有"长命富贵"、"五子登科"、"福寿双全"、"状元及第"等，这些四字吉祥铭文镜均为楷书，每字置于一方框内，自上向下，从右到左释读。本书收录明清铜镜25面，双鱼镜2面，龙纹镜1面，人物多宝镜3面，铭文镜15面，仿镜2面。

龙纹镜，本书收录1面，为洪武二十二年铭云龙镜，直径11厘米，边厚0.6厘米，重327克，该镜为圆形，山形钮。钮右侧一龙腾于云海之中，龙首在钮下，身躯蟠曲于上，前肢伸展，一后肢与龙尾缠绕，另一后肢仅露五爪。龙首前有云气缠绕。左侧一方框内有铭文"洪武二十二年正月日造"。素宽平缘。镜背纹饰均采用浮雕技法，将龙腾于祥云之中的景象刻画的惟妙惟肖。

人物多宝镜，是明代最具特色的镜类。纹饰中常见的有"八宝"，分别是轮、螺、伞、盖、花、罐、鱼、肠，又称法轮、法螺、宝伞、白盖、莲花、宝罐、金鱼、盘肠。但铜镜上用作装饰的图案，往往不局限于这八宝，增加了钱文、祥云、灵芝、卷轴书画、银锭、元宝、犀角、方胜、珊瑚、磬、鹿、梅花等，成为"多宝"或者"杂宝"镜。这些多宝寓意吉祥如意、福禄双全、健康长寿等。本书收录的一面明代人物多宝镜，直径7.4厘米，边厚0.1厘米，重56克。形制为圆形，镜体极薄，银锭钮。纹饰由上至下分五

个层次排列：最上方一展翅曲颈仙鹤，两侧各饰一对犀角；第二层中为方胜，两侧各有宝珠三粒；第三层即钮的两侧各饰一银锭；第四层为二书卷；最下方正中一座聚宝盆，上盛仙果什物，两侧方胜与宝钱。二、三、四层外侧各一人，面向中心，手持宝物。

随着西方玻璃镜的流行，铜镜发展到清代已经全面衰落，不但纹饰简单，工艺粗糙，产量也大为减少。本书收录清代铜镜2面，双喜五蝠纹带柄镜是清代流行的新纹饰，寓意幸福美满。蝠与福谐音，五蝠谐音五福多指福、禄、寿、喜、财，是一种吉祥纹饰。

苕溪薛惠公造铭文镜，方形，无钮。镜背铸16字楷书铭文，"方正而明，万里无尘。水天一色，犀照群伦"。左下角铸篆书"苕溪"圆形章和"薛惠公造"方形章各一枚。素宽平缘。薛惠公，名晋侯，字惠公，号苕溪，清乾隆时人，以铸镜素有佳名。薛家是铸镜世家，明清时期，以铸造铜镜精良、品质上乘而声名远播。明代《乌程县志》说："湖之薛镜驰名。薛，杭人，而业于湖。以磨镜必用湖水为佳。"薛惠公更是薛家之登峰造极者，其所制铜镜极富盛名。

综观中国铜镜四千年的发展历史，每个时期的铜镜都被打上了深深地时代烙印，在见方大小的铜镜上，我们隐约可以看到四千年中国历史的沧桑变化。同时，铜镜以其独特的制作工艺、构思巧妙的纹饰样式、典型的题材来源、强烈的艺术感染力在中华文明的宝库中熠熠生辉。虽然在历史的潮流中，铜镜逐渐远离了我们的生活，但它们的神韵却不会因时间的流逝而泯灭，将永留于我们的心中。

I

Bengbu city is located in the north-central of Anhui Province. Geogrophical position is east longitude 117 ° 11 '- 117 ° 31',north latitude 32 ° 49 '- 33 ° 01'. Throughout the north,it borders with Suzhou City,Suixi,Sixian and Lingbi County,connects to Fengyang County and Huainan City throughout the South.Adjacent to Mingguang City and Sihong County of Jiangsu Province from the east,borders with Mengcheng County and Fengtai City on the west.The Tientsin pukow railway runs through the city from north to south,Huaihe River flows from west to east across the city. There are three countries in Bengbu City,Huaiyuan,Guzhen and Wuhe,and four districts include the Dragon Lake,Bengshan,Yuhui and Huaishang.The total area of this city is 5952 square kilometers and population is about 3583100.

In ancient time,Huai River flowed from Jing mountain pass of Huaiyuan country to Bengbu region, with slow,clear water and dense grass,abounded with freshwater mussel and pearl.The Yu Gong of Shang Book says, "Nearby Huai River there was a kind of blue stone can be made of inverted bell,and in the river there were lots of fish and freshwater mussel with pearl."Fengyang Prefecture Records written in Qing Dynasty says, "Bengbu is aplace famous for collecting pearl in ancient time and located 160 miles southwest of Lingbi."Therefore, Bengbu is also called "Pearl city".

Bengbu is one of the important areas of human life and production with a long history since ancient time. According to archaeological discoveries,the trail of human activities has been found in Bengbu area at about thirty thousand years ago; seven thousand years ago Shuangdun Culture has revealed the dawn of civilization; four thousand years ago Tushan Country settled here. Ai Gong of Master Zuo's Spring and Autumn Annals says, "Yu met thousands of princes with jade and silk at Tu Mountain", which means Tushan Yuhui Village site.

The Huan Yi people once gathered and lived here in Xia,Shang and Zhou Dynasty.To the Spring and Autumn Period,Bengbu belonged to the Zhongli country,and ever was part of Xu Fang, Lu, song, Wu, Yue and Chu country During the Warring States Period.

After the founding of the Qin Dynasty,it was under control of Jiujiang and Sishui country according to the system of prefectures and counties.The north side of Huai River in Bengbu area belonged to Pei country and the opposite belonged to Huainan which changed named as Jiujiang in Han Dynasty.

Wei country owned Bengbu in the Three Kingdoms Period. The north part of Huai River belonged to Qiao country and the other part belonged to Huainan.After that, Bengbu's organization system changed frequently because of lasting war from Jin Dynasty to the Northern and Southern Dynasties.

From Sui Dynasty to Kaiyuan 21th year of Tang Dynasty(733),Huainan state supervised south part of Huai River in Bengbu area,and Henan state monitored the opposite one.The Five Dynasties changed regime and system in disorder often, until Xiande fifth year of Later Zhou Dynasty(958) the whole Bengbu region has a complete integration.As the boundary,north of the Huai River came within the jurisdiction of Xuzhou,while the other part under the jurisdiction of Haozhou.

In Northern Song Dynasty,north part of Huai River in Bengbu belonged to a newly-stalled country named Lingbi which under the jurisdiction of Huainan East Road,Suzhou. Meanwhile,there was only Zhongli country on the south side of Huai River which belonged to Huainan West Road,Haozhou. From the beginning of Southern Song Dynasty to Baoyou fifth year(1257),western Bengbu was reset as Jingshan country which under the jurisdiction of Huaiyuan army in Huainan West Road.Up to Xianchun seventh year(1271),Wuhe country was set in northeast Bengbu,belonged to Huainan army in Huainan East Road.During the period Southern Song Dynasty against Jin Dynasty,today's Guzhen country was leaded separately by Qi country Suzhou,Lingbi country and Hong country Sizhou at the frist time,and then by country of Suzhou,Lingbi,Jingshan and Wuhe.

To Yuan Dynasty,Huaiyuan army was canceled in Zhiyuan 28th year(1291). Jingshan country was renamed Huaiyuan which belonged to Haozhou.Today's downtown area belonged to Huaiyuan from the west and Zhongli from the east;today's Guzhen country was leaded separately by Suzhou,Lingbi,Wuhe and Huaiyuan,among which,Huaiyuan was charged by Sizhou.

Hongwu years in Ming Dynasty,Zhongli county was renamed Zhongli and Linhuai, also added Fengyang country;today's downtown area belonged to Huaiyuan from the west and Fengyang from the east;today's Guzhen country was leaded separately by Suzhou,Huaiyuan,Lingbi,Wuhe and Fengyang.Haozhou was first changed into Linhao Palace and then Fengyang Palace,the whole territory belonged to Fengyang Palace.

The system of Ming Dynasty was used the same in Qing Dynasty. Wuhe belonged to Sizhou which broke away from Fengyang Palace until the year of Yongzheng.The main office of Fengyang country was quartered at Bengbu,meanwhile,the three country department was set up as an independent administrative region which belonged to Fengyang,Anhui

province in the year of Tongzhi second(1863),Qing Dynasty,concluding of west of Macungou in Fengyang,east of Xijiagou in Huaiyuan and Houlou in Lingbi.

Bengbu formally established as a city in January 1, 1947, under control directly of Anhui Province,which also is the first city in Anhui province.

II

The bronze mirror which serves as an indispensable tool for reflecting people's face and readjusting their appearance is commonly used by ancient people.It's not only a practical commodity,but even an art treasure of cultural heritage,including one shiny side serves as reflecting people's face,and a decorative side with exquisite design and carved inscriptions.

About the origin and transformation of bronze mirror,the famous scholar Liang Shangchun pointed out in the book of *Research On Ancient Mirror*, "still water—still water in a bronze basin—empty basin without water—shiny copper—copper with a knob on its back side—mirror without design on back side—ground motif without design but painting—without painting but cast with graphic—cast with inscription".Thus,the origin of bronze mirror was evolved from still water's function of reflecting people's face.The bronze mirror has a long history in China,according to current archaeological discoveries, it appeared to Qijia Culture dating back to 4000 years ago for the first time.The two round-shaped bronze mirrors with knob and design on the back side which unearthed from Qijia Culture in 1970s, were the first step about "round plate with knob" in history and had an important influence on bronze mirror's development.

The Shang and Zhou Dynasties were the golden period of the bronze. compared with a great variety of other splendid bronzes,the bronze mirror only unearthed just 20-odd and found mainly in the area of upper reaches of the Yellow River. The reason for this is that the bronze mirror did not form its own complete procedure yet and on its early period.

The Spring and Autumn Period and the Warring period were the epidemic stage of bronze mirror which had a quick development and brilliant achievements.During this period,the bronze mirror with light weigh,exquisite design and flowing line which on behalf of new style instead of simple and austere style in last Dynasty.The Han Dynasty was the peak period for bronze mirror,Catalogue On Ancient Mirror says,"Ingenious depicting,glamorous writing and elegant rhetoric only can be seen at the same time is on the bronze mirror". This description

generalized the characteristics of Han Mirror in a properly way.The bronze mirror grown sluggish delay during the Three Kingdoms Period,Two Jin Dynasties and Southern-Northern Dynasties.After a period of downturn,it came to the prosperity time on Sui and Tang Dynasties.Tang Mirror was different from neither Warring State Mirror in light weigh,nor Han Mirror in formal style.It had a great breakthrough in both shape and theme than the previous dynasties with variety of types,new shapes,innovative technology and modern design showing up,just like the open dynasty,Tang.Since the Five,Song,Jin and Yuan Dynasties,the bronze mirror fading and withdrew from historical stage gradually,and finally replaced by glass mirror to Ming and Qing Dynasties.

According to current unearthed bronze mirrors,on the point of shape,even though there were mirror with shape of square,flower,handle and so on,round plate with knob has been the main shape and one of the most important features of bronze mirror all the time in history.As to the normal theme and design cast on bronze mirror, although generations have their own characteristics, the unique fauna is always an important subject. From the serpentine interlaced hydras and serpents in Warring State to dragon on clouds in Ming and Qing Dynasties,the image of dragon never disappear on bronze mirror as the totem of the Chinese nation.Today,while the bronze mirror withdrew from the stage of history,but its spirit will never vanish due to the passage of time and alway shiny in Chinese Civilization Art Treasure.

III

The Spring and Autumn and Warring States period was the mature and developing period in the history of the development of Chinese ancient bronze mirror,which was the transition stage of bronze mirror from simple and young to maturity,and also the important period of casting center migrating from north to south.During this period,the bronze mirror had a great and complete development on both casting technology and variety compared to previous dynasties such as Xia,Shang and Zhou.

Mirror with inscription of "shan" character was a popular kind during Waring State Period,usually classified as three,four,five and six "shan"mirror according to the number of "shan" characters.Among which,mirror with four "shan" characters was the most one.Mirror with inscription of four "shan"characters which was unearthed at Bali Bridge Tomb at western suburbs of Bengbu city in1973,is found in the earliest times in this region up to now.The mirror is round in shape. It has a knob with four-string design on a square base.The design on the back consist of ground motif and main motif. The ground is decorated with design of feather-like pattern as ground motif,on which there are four consistent groups of petal extend from center part,each group has two pieces of petal,on top of each petal connects with a wooden club shaped long-leaf pattern which arranged in anticlockwise.The back side of bronze mirror is divided into four pieces by design of four groups of petal and long-leaf pattern,each piece cast a left-handed and slender strokes "shan"inscription. There is one piece of petal decorate on the right rib of each "shan". There are 12 petals and 4 long-leaves, among which,all the petals are connected with narrow band pattern.The mirror has a broad and rolling rim without design.This mirror with delicate casting,thin and light mirror body,intricate and elegant decorations,natural and smart "Shan" characters,is a typical mirror of the Chu State.

The Han Dynasty was the prosperous period in ancient China as an unified,unlit ethnic and feudal nation, and its feudal economy presented an unprecedented prosperity.With the development of economy,manufacture technique had a great improvement on both scale and level,the process of metal casting grown fast as well. The bronze mirror was cast the most among the bronze productions in Han Dynasty. The quantity was much higher than Warring State Period,meanwhile, the style and artistic expression improved a lot. There is a large amount of the Han bronze mirror among mirrors collected in the museum,occupying about thirty percent.Forty-three mirrors of Han Dynasty are listed in the book,with design of linked arc,gambling,four nipples,several nipples,beast,bird,flower, portrait of deities and inscription of band.

Mirror with inscription and design of linked arcs is one of the bronze mirrors which were unearthed in a great number and were popular in Han Dynasty,from the middle Western Han Dynasty to the early Eastern Han Dynasty.The feature of the mirror is with linked arc design on inner part of base and inscription band on outer part,which formed the major motif together.According to the inscription, divided into "Ri Guang" and "Zhao Ming", there are two mirrors with inscription of "Ri Guang", eight mirrors with inscription of "Zhao Ming", one mirror with linked arcs design and inscription of "Ri You Xi".The two mirrors with inscription of "Ri Guang" are 7cm diameter,have a thin body, and are made in rough method,with same inscription of "Jian Ri Zhi Guang,Tian Xia Da Ming".The "Ri Guang" mirror in our museum has a bigger shape and a heavier body than mirror with inscription of "Ri Guang" ,made in regular procedure.The mirror is round in shape,it has a round knob on a round base.Outside the base is a band of eight linked arcs inside,two bands of fine-toothed pattern which with a circle band of inscription inside.The complete inscription should be

"Nei Qing Zhi Yi Zhao Ming,Guang Hui Xiang Fu Xi Ri Yue,Xin Hu Yang Er Yuan Zhong,Ran Yong Sai Er Bu Zhi",but because of the different sizes of the mirror, the reduce of the inscription often reduced or omit, in general, was controlled in a range.There is another situation, "Er" which without any practical literature significance added in words to make up the vacancy of the words. Mirror with linked arcs design and inscription of "Ri You Xi" unearthed at a tile tomb,Long Kang Xiang Bridge Commune in Bengbu City in1983,with 15.1cm diameter.The mirror is round in shape. It has a round knob on a base with kaki calyx.Outside the base is a band of raised string pattern and eight linked arcs pattern inward,inside the band are simple decorations formed by short lines.Outside the band are two bands of fine-toothed pattern with a circle of inscription.According to archaeological discoveries,this kind of mirror has a larger size than mirror with inscription of "Ri Guang" and "Zhao Ming",mostly with 14cm diameter at least and popular in later time.

The mirror with gambling design is also called the mirror with standard design.Another name,the mirror with design of "T. L. V"is given by foreign scholars because of the regular decoration of "T. L. V"on the mirror.It's generally agreed that the gambling design originated in six gambling chess game in Han Dynasty. Gambling is a game bet win and lose which was very popular in a great range from nobility to common people in Qin and Han society.The making procedure of the bronze mirror was quite unified then,mostly round knob, round base or design of kaki calyx. Outside the base a band of square formed by double lines concave surface. Inside the square there are designs or inscriptions.Four groups "T. L. V"gambling pattern divided into eight parts,each part is adored with deities,winged men,bird,beast and geometric patterns,between the bands often decorated with inscription band.The mirror has a broad rim decorated with wave pattern formed by double lines,jagged pattern,cloud and steam pattern.The gambling design frist appeared in the region of the Emperor Wu of the Han Dynasty,but widely used between the late Western Han Dynasty and the early Eastern Han Dynasty. The bronze mirror reached a peak period in the region of Wang Mang,with delicate design,high quality and advanced technology.It began decay in the late period of the middle Eastern Han Dynasty,with simplified pattern and rough technology,and finally disappeared in the early Wei and Jin Dynasties.The gambling design is a kind of pattern which is the best and popular for the longest time in Han Mirror.

There are fourteen bronze mirrors with gambling design listed in this book.An Eastern Han Dynasty bronze mirror with 4.5cm diameter,0.5cm thickness of rim,818 gram weigh which unearthed at tombs of Wan Long Auto Parts Factory in Yuhui Region of Bengbu City in 2009.The mirror is round in shape.It

has a round knob on a base with kaki calyx design.Outside the base are two squares,one is formed by raised string pattern,the other one is formed by double lines concave surface.Between the squares there are design of twelve nipples with round base and inscription of twelve Earthly Branches interphase around the knob.Outside the concave surface square there are eight nipples with round base and four groups of "T. L. V" gambling design which divided the mirror into four zones,each corner of the square decorated with Green Dragon,White Tiger,Scarlet Bird and Somber Warrior. While each deity adored with a mythical beast,the deity and the mythical beast standing face to face separated by a "V" design.Outside that is a band of inscription "Shang Fang Zuo Jing Zhen Da Qiao,Shang You Xian Ren Bu Zhi Lao,Ke Yin Yu Quan Ji Shi Zao,Fu You Tian Xia Ao Si Hai"□It's a classic bronze mirror with inscription of "Shang Fang" and design of four deities and gambling with delicate mold and exquisite pattern. "Shang Fang"was the department that made production only used for Royal in Han Dynasty which under the charge of department named "Shao Fu".Royal-made mirror was used only by royalty with high quality and exquisite pattern.At that time,there were many civil craftsmen made false mirror with rough technology under the name of Royal-made.

The main feature of bronze mirror with design of four nipples and animals is the design of serpent,flying birds,animal,four deities and so on which cast outside the base between the four nipples.According to the different patterns around between the four nipples,the bronze mirror divided into mirror with design of four nipples and four serpents,mirror with design of four nipples and birds and animals,mirror with design of four nipples and four deities.There are three mirrors with design of four nipples and four serpents,four mirrors with design of four nipples and birds and animals.The bronze mirror with design of four nipples and four serpents which unearthed from Han tomb,Tianhe Commune in 1990,with round shape and a round knob on a round base. Outside the base is a band of raising string pattern.Between the base and raising string pattern are simple designs formed by short lines. Outside that are two bands of fine-toothed pattern,between the pattern distribute equidistantly design of four nipples with round base,in the spaced decorated with four hook-shaped serpents which has same style on both side.Each side of the serpent has a bird. The mirror has a broad and flat rim without design.Serpent is a famous creature lives in mountains in ancient legend, is considered to be a simplified pattern of the image of dragon. The Note Record Strange says, a serpent takes five hundreds years to change into a Jiao,a Jiao needs one thousand years to change into a dragon.

Mirrors with portraits of deities and beasts have two

kinds,one is mirror with design of mythical creature,the other one is mirror with portrait of deities.widely used in Yangtze River between the late period of middle Eastern Han Dynasty and Wei,Jin,the Southern and Northern Dynasties.The ground motif decorated on the mirror like deities portrait,dragon and tiger pattern are casted by relief style,which mainly from the myth and folklore with deep moral and ingenious conception.There are two mirrors with portraits of deities and beasts,one is mirror with portrait,the other is mirror with design of beasts.Mostly,the ground motif of mirror with portrait is the Royal Lord of the East and the Royal Lady of the West sitting with attendant standing by,also decorated with carriage,birds,beasts,wing-men and so on.The mirror is round in shape with a round knob,there are band of inscriptions,and patterns of clouds,birds,animals,jagged and waves decorated on the rim.Mirror with portraits of deities and beasts was a new type of mirror in the Eastern Han Dynasty,the design,style and relief technology marked the new stage of bronze mirror's development.

The mirror with design of dragon and tiger divided into three kinds,mirror with design of single dragon,mirror with design of single tiger and mirror with design of dragon and tiger.Mainly popular in the late period of middle Eastern Han Dynasty until to Wei,Jin,Southern and Northern Dynasties. There are two mirrors with design of dragon and tiger in the book,the dragon and tiger facing each other against the big round knob in high relief.The mirror is round in shape.There are five mirrors with design of three tigers.The bronze mirror with design of three tigers unearthed at Huaiyuan Country in 1994 is 11cm diameter,1.5cm thick of rim and 364 gram weigh. The mirror is round in shape.It has a round knob on a round base.Outside the base are three tigers in high relief circled with the knob,among which,two tigers are facing each other,the third one followed behind which decorated with big nipple on body to protrude.The three tigers are stretching and pedaling.Outside the tiger pattern is a band of inscription "Long Shi Zuo Jing Si Yi (Fu),Duo He Jun Jia Ren Min Xi,Hu Qiang Zhen (Mie) Tian Xia Fu,Shi Jie".Outside the inscription is surrounded with fine-toothed band.The broad rim is decorated with saw pattern and wave pattern formed by double lines.

The Wei,Jin,Southern and Northern Dynasties is a period which regime changed frequently the most in Chinese history,the development of economy and culture during this period affected particularly due to long time feudal separatism and unstopping war.The manufacturing of bronze mirror also had a certain degree of combat and came to a temporary decline period.There are two mirrors made in this period listed in the book.One of the them is mirror with inscription of Wei Zhi San Gong and design of dragon and phoenix,the mirror is 11cm diameter,0.27cm thick of rim and weighs 160 gram.The mirror is round in shape,it has a round knob on a round base.Above and below the knob are double lines with inscriptions cast in,while "Wei Zhi" was above the knob and "San Gong" below it.Left side of the knob decorated a phoenix with "S" style,meanwhile a dragon with "S"style on right side.Outside is a band of fine-toothed pattern,the rim is broad without design.Some scholars believe that this kind of mirror derived from mirror with design of dragon and phoenix with double heads which popular in Eastern Han Dynasty.

The founding of Sui Dynasty brought the end of north and south split situation which had been last for over 300 years. Then the following up Tang Dynasty with an unified country,the feudal politics,economy and culture grown in prosper,handicraft industry also also showing a thriving scene,which promoted the development of the bronze mirror's making technology a lot.The Tang Mirror has its own style in the shape,material and casting technology,it's the peak of Chinese bronze mirror. Just like the open dynasty,Tang Mirror was different from neither Warring State Mirror in light weigh,nor Han Mirror in formal style,the shape not only in round,but also water chestnut shape and mallow shape.The theme of the mirror got rid of the influence of Huang Lao and God,close to life more.The vibrant and energetic patterns of flying phoenix and bird,fresh flowers and jumping animals are the mark of peace and stable society.

There are 22 Tang mirrors listed in the book,most of them are mirror with auipicious beasts and mirror with flower design.Among the mirrors,there are 13mirrors with auspicious beasts,eight mirrors with flowers design,with design of beasts,beasts and grapes,beasts and phoenix,birds,flowers,rosette and legendary incident of Gods,covering round shape,water chestnut shape and mallow shape.

Mirror with design of auspicious beasts and grapes also called mirror with sea beast and grape.From the record of Jin Shisuo we know that the pattern of grapes came from western regions and grapes were brought by Zhang Qian to China in the reign of Emperor Wu of the Han Dynasty.According to historical records,there were already grapes planting in Shanglin Parkland at that time.When Tang Dynasty,grape was widely planted and grape pattern began to popular,while the auspicious beasts decoration has a long historical tradition,it's prevailed from Six Dynasties to Sui and early Tang Dynasties. The mirror with design of auspicious beasts is the combine of two popular patterns right then,and became a new kind of Tang Dynasty unique mirror.There are two mirrors with design of

auspicious beasts and grapes listed in the book,both are round in shape.The mirror combine auspicious beasts and grapes together,also decorated with birds and flowers,which showing up a vivid and lively picture:propitious cloud and auspicious beasts are running and playing in the sea,magpie flying around the branches full of grapes with graceful and beautiful pose. There is almost no blank on the mirror,only little branches and vines added into the gap with decoration of butterfly and bird in different poses and with different expressions shuttling among them.The mirror is thriving and magnificent.

The mirror with design of magpie circled the flowers collected in our museum is 10cm diameter,0.5cm thickness of rim and weight 175gram.The mirror is in water chestnut shape with eight petals,it has a round knob.Outside the knob there are four birds and four branches of flower alternated with each other.Four birds divided into two groups,one group of two magpies spreading the wings and tails and flying,the other group of two geese standing on the feet and wings closed. Between the four birds there are two branches of flowers in different shapes distribute symmetrically.On the rim of the mirror,there are four flying bees and butterflies alternate with four interlocking flowers with two leaves and one bud.The motif design create a quiet and peaceful picture,which truly reflect a glory of the Tang Dynasty,expressing people's love for life and peace at that time.

The mirror with design of interlocking flowers and birds collected from citizen in 1975 is 21.5cm diameter,0.5cm thickness of rim and weight 1252 gram.The mirror is round in shape,it has a round knob on a petal-shaped base.Outside the base there are four interlocking flowers with five leaves and one bud circled the knob,below each flower has a magpie with wings spreading or head turning around.Between the four branches decorated a flower with two leaves and a bud. The whole mirror designed well-proportioned,various but not chaotic,birds with vivid shapes,flowers in full blossom,shows up a thriving scene.

There is one mirror with design of Zhen Zi play the zither listed in the book,the mirror is in shape of eight-petal mallow. It has a tortoise-shaped knob on a base with design of lotus leaf.On the left side of the knob is adored with a man wearing a top hat and wide clothes with belts,sitting before a censer table and bamboos forest behind,playing the zither.On the right side of the knob is adored with a phoenix spreading wings and tail, dancing on a stone,above the phoenix are two trees. The knob is decorated with sun and moon in the cloud on the top and stone,mountain,pool with ripples at the bottom.In the pool is adored with a stretching bent lotus leaf with a tortoise

on it,which formed the knob.There is no exact determine about the meaning which the mirror reflect.Some scholar believe that Zhen Zi is the short one for Zhen Xiao Zi,while Fei Shuang is also mamed Lv Ji Cao,one of the famous twelve melodies of ancient zither which telling the story about Yin Boqi was exiled in the wild by the King Xuan of the Zhou.

Yin Boqi,the son of Yin Jifu who was one of the ministers belongs to the King Xuan of the Zhou, was a famous filial son and good at melody. After his birth-mother died,his step-mother wanted her own son BoGua inherited the title and property,so she set him up.The woman told his father that Boqi teased her and let his father hide to watch.The step-mother caught a poison bee and hid it in her sleeve,then she released it when Boqi gave his respect to her.Boqi disregard the danger and helped to caught the poison bee,so he put his hands on the mother's clothes.His father did not see the poison bee because of the long distance,so he believed the step-mother's words,thought Boqi was doing bad things to the step-mother. He drove Boqi out of home.Yin Boqi didn't want to argue with that,so he took his beloved zither and forced to leave his home.

Yin Boqi was alone in the wild,hungry and cold.Thought of his grievances,so he made a piece of desolate zither melody named Lv Qin Cao(also named Fei Shuang Cao).Right now the King Xuan of the Zhou was patrolling the country and passing by here with the company of Yin Jifu,heard the melody and said: "The singer must be a dutiful son with badly treatment."Yin Jinfu heard his son's melody,felt doubt and regret,so he sent someone to found Yin Boqi and the truth came out.The father killed the step-wife with angry and brought BoQi back home.At last,the father and the son got together again.

After the downfall of the Tang Dynasty,China entered a chaotic period of the Five Dynasties,the Ten Kingdoms period,Liao,Song,Jin and Yuan Dynasties.The founding of Northern Song Dynasty brought the end of chaotic situation of the Central Plain,but with the rising of minority nationalities Liao,Western Xia and Jin,lead to a political upheaval.With the Northern Song,Liao and Western Xia coexisting during the Northern Song Dynasty,and the Southern Song and Jin confronting each other during the Southern Song Dynasty. Because of frequent wars and lack of raw materials,the bronze mirror making collapsed.The unity of the Yan Dynasty make a very complex situation in this period,the regional political, economic development showing a imbalanced prospect. With the change of political suiation and different national traditions,this bronze mirror during this period also has significant age difference and national style.

There are four bronze mirrors in the Five Dynasties listed in the book.The Sheng-fang mirror with inscription of "Liu Si Xun Zao",which was unearthed at Qiu Jia Hummock,Huai Guang Country,Bengbu City in 1986,is made by Dou Sheng.On the mirror there are inscriptions cast by the maker.The mirror is 16.1cm diameter,0.25cm thickness of the rim and weigh 342 gram.The mirror is round in shape and has a round knob. Outside the knob is a big square formed by a band of design of double beads,in the square decorate with linked line design. Between the two groups of linked beads design are cast four inscriptions on both left and right side space: Sheng Fang Jing Mian,Liu Si Xun Zao.While on the top and bottom sides of space decorated with four groups of flowers design respectively. At the four corners of the square decorated with money design. Outside the square are covered with full of turtle patterns.The major motif ends with two bands of linked beads,and the rim is broad without design.

Song Mirror,with light body and simple ornament,focus more on practical use than luxury.The mirrors are mainly round shape,square,arc,rhombus and mirror with handle also exist.The decoration on mirror back tends to be realistic pattern, with painting styles. The patterns are more about flowers,birds,fish,worms,as well as crouching dragons,serpents,flying phoenix.The painted animals and plants are vivid and various.On the melting and coining part,tin decreases,lead increases,the changed alloy transformed the quality and color which deeply affected the making of later bronze mirror.This book collects twenty-three mirrors of Song and Jin Dynasty,including design of flowers,double fish,flower and birds,legendary incident of deity,etc,and Hou Zhou Mirror with inscription.

Mirror with interlocking flowers and leaves,the major motif are of various kinds of flower spray and petals,dealt by shallow fine relief method.The thin spray and petals crouches together,forming delicate pictures.Mirror with four interlocking flowers,collected from Bengbu City in 1975,with the diameter of 14.8cm,thickness of 0.1cm and weight of 200 grams.It was in shape of Ya character. It has bridge-shaped knob on a base with design of flower petal. Around the base are four flowers,the flowers are against the inner corner of Ya character.It presents a delicate picture of spray and petals,with a strong sense of reality and rhythm.

Mirror with double phoenixes of this museum is of 26cm diameter,round shape and round knob.Two phoenixes flying around the knob in same shape.Both phoenixes have low crests above the heads,thin and crooked necks,stretched wings,rich feather and long empennage.The phoenixes are spaced with clouds pattern.Outside the major motif is a band of raised string pattern. The mirror has a narrow rim.The phoenixes feather is delineated carefully,true and vivid.The whole painting is of thin lines and delicate.It makes people feel relax and romantic,from which we can see the masterpiece of the craftsmen in Song Dynasty.

Huzhou Mirror is the most famous style.There are in shape of mallow,Ya character,square,peach and so on.This book collected eight Huzhou mirrors with inscription,respectively,five mirrors in shape of mallow,one mirror in shape of Ya character,two mirrors in shape of peach.The main inscriptions are "Huzhou Zhen Shi Jia Nian Er Shu Zhao Zi","Huzhou Yi Feng Qiao Shi Jia,Zhen Zheng Yi Se Qing Tong Zhao Zi", etc..It is to be noted that, people called mirror "Zhao Zi" in Song Dynasty.That is due to Song has a rigid taboo,while the emperor Zhao Kuangyin's ancestor was Jing,people had to overt the use of "Jing",and then called mirror "Zhao Zi" or "Jian Zi".In the 33th year of Shao Xing period,the government declared to free people from using the word "Jing",but in the first year of Shao Xi period,the taboo was remade.So during this period,people could use "Jing" which refers to the mirror. Huzhou mirror could date back to late North Song Dynasty,and was popular from early to middle South Song Dynasty.It was mainly prevalent in the south area.In the end of North Song Dynasty,many northerners migrated to the south to avoid wars. Then the economic center also transformed to the south area.At that time,cities like Huzhou, Raozhou, Lin'anfu, Ping'anfu and so on,were famous places for the mirror-making.Huzhou mirror has little pattern;it was made only with craftsman's name and prices,often named with "Zhen" or "Zhen Zheng",to show its authenticity and prevent fake.

Mirror with pattern of legendary incident of Xu You and Chao Fu is of 18cm diameter,0.8cm thick of rim and 1,250 gram weight,round in shape and has a round knob with a flat top.The half part above the knob is adored with several lofty mountains,on the top of middle mountain planting a tree with branches hanging till the hillside.The below part is casting with two talking people,one is sitting,the other one is holding a cattle.The rim without design is broad and has a flat surface. This is alluded to an ancient tales: In ancient times,the leader of the tribe union was elected by Shanrang system.Yao especially paid attention to the candidate's mass basis when considering his successor.He was heard of that Chao Fu and Xu You of Yang City(today's Shanxi,Hongdong)were great sages,and paid visits to them.At the first visiting to Chao Fu,Chao refused;then to Xu You,Xu also denied and hermit-ted to farmland in Jiu Qi Hill of Hongdong.While Yao persistently went to Xu You and persuaded him succeed the leadership of Jiu Zhou,Xu You felt being insulted and run to the river to wash his "dirty" ears.

Xu You was washing his ears by the river,while his good friend Chao Fu,who secluded on the tree,took his cow to drink water.When Chao Fu got know the reason why Xu You washing his ears,he said, "This owe to you,for if you want to withdraw from the secular life,why not be a hermit?Now your ears are dirty,the water becomes dirty too,my spotless cow would not drink the dirty water."After Chao Fu finished his words,he took the cow to the upstream for drinking......This is the story of "Xu You and Chao Fu".

The mirror-making faded in Late Tang and Five Dynasties,but prospered in Jin Dynasty with various styles.Jin is a north sovereignty nation of Nvzhen,reflecting on the mirror cultural variety,merging with rugged customs and habits,which made the mirror greatly different from Huzhou Mirror.The administration was extremely rigid by Jin government,it banned private from coining bronze,so the bronze mirror often got government inscription or permission on the mirror edge. There were also new types and subject of Jin mirror,mostly were mirrors with design of double fish and legendary incident. This book collects nine bronze mirrors of Jin Dynasty,mainly are mirror with design of double fish,makara,flower mirror and legendary incident.

Mirror with handle and makara pattern,is in shape of a peach and has a long handle.There is a makara flying up over the rolling sea.On the top of the mirror back, there is a crescent in the sky.The raised rim showing no design is narrow.The word makara is translated by its Sanskrit pronunciation.Makara is a river elvish in India's tale,like the river god in China.After makara being transmitted to China,it has been reinterpreted by Chinese Buddhist,and got the image of Dragon-like head and fish-like body.Makara becomes a fish god and is the Buddha's transformation in water form.

This book collects two mirrors with pattern of legendary incident. One is Wu buffaloes pant for mistaking moon as sun,which is round in shape and has a round knob.In the middle of the knob is adored with a square formed by single line.Outside are clouds and crescent in the sky.The sky merge with sea and moving clouds,which take the most part of the mirror back.At both right and left sides of the knob,standing a god,holding treasures.Below the knob is a buffalo,looking up with panting sound.The rim without design is broad and has a flat surface.The delineating lines are alluded to Jiang Huai buffaloes pant for taking moon as sun: the buffaloes of south region are afraid of hot,and mistaking moon as sun,so pant when seeing the moon.Later,when afraid of similar things,people call it "Wu buffalo pant the moon".

The Ming and Qing mirror-making was more developed than Song era.The mirror got heavier bodies and more delicate craftsmanship.Many bronze mirrors that modeled after

Han Dynasty Style are made,while mirror with auspicious inscription was also very famous.The main inscriptions are "Chang Ming Fu Gui", "Wu Zi Deng Ke", "Fu Shou Shuang Quan", "Zhuang Yuan Ji Di",etc..The characters are written by regular script,one word with one rectangle,read from the above to bottom,right to left.This book collects twenty-five bronze mirrors of Ming and Qing Dynasty,among them are two mirrors with design of double fish,one mirror with dragon pattern,three mirrors with design of figures and treasures,fourteen mirrors with inscription,two imitation of the mirror.

Mirror with design of figures and treasures is the most characteristic mirror type of Ming Dynasty.The decorations on the mirror are usually Eight Treasures,which refers to wheel, spiral shell, umbrella, lid, flower, tin, fish, auspicious knot.But the decorations are not confined to these. There are also patterns of coin, propitious cloud, glossy ganoderma, scroll painting and books, silver ingot, treasure, rhinoceros horn,interlocking lozenge, coral, chime stone, deer, plum blossom, etc.,so we called mirror like multi-treasure mirrors or miscellaneous-treasure mirrors.These patterns of treasure indicates everything goes well,happiness,health,longevity and so on.This book collect one mirror with design of figures and treasures of Ming Dynasty,with a 7.4cm diameter, 0.1cm thick and 56 gram weight.The mirror is round in shape,has a light body and a silver ingot shaped knob.The decoration on its back side is divided into five layers:at the top layer is a crane adored with a pair of rhinoceros horns on its both sides,which is stretching wings and bending neck;the second layer is intersecting lozenge with decoration of three treasure beads on both sides of the lozenge;the third layer has two silver ingots on both sides of the knob;the fourth layer indudes two book scroll. At the middle part of the bottom is a treasure basin with fruits and treasures inside,and decorations of intersecting lozenge and coins on both sides of the basin.Both outer sides of middle part

This book collects one mirror with dragon pattern,which was amirror with inscription of "Hong Wu Er Shi Er Nian" and design of cloud and dragon.It is of 11 am diameter, 0.6-cm thick and 327-gram weight,with round shape and a mountain-shaped knob.At the right side of the knob is a dragon flying in the clouds with head hide under the knob,body curling on the knob,forelimbs stretching,one hind limb twisting with its tail,the other hind limb exposing five paws only.There are lots of clouds and steam before the dragon's head.At the left side of the knob is a rectangle with inscription of "Hong Wu Er Shi Er Nian Zheng Yue Ri Zao".The broad rim without design has a plat surface.The ornamentation of the mirror back uses the craftsmanship of relief sculpture,which makes the dragon vivid.

is a person standing face the center and holding treasures.

As western glass mirror was prevalent,the production of bronze mirror decreased, and faded away.In the Qing Dynasty,the bronze mirror declined,with raw materials in a low quality,simple patterns and rough technology.This book collects two mirrors of Qing Dynasty.Mirror with handle and design of double "Xi" and five bats was a new popular kind in Qing Dynasty,indicating happiness and fullness.The bat pronounced the same as happiness in Chinese,so,five bates usually means five happiness,which were seen as happiness, luckiness, longevity, delight and wealth.

Mirror with inscription of "Zhao Xi Xue Hui Gong Zao" is of square shape and no knob.On the back of mirror,there are 16 regular words "Fang Zheng Er Mig,Wan Li Wu Chen,Shui Tian Yi Se,Xi Zhao Qun Lun".On the left bottom, there are round badge with two seal characters "Shao Xi" and square badge with "Xue Hui Gong Zao".The mirror without design is broad and has a flat surface.Xuehui Gong's name is Jinhou,also called Tiaoxi.He was a man of Qianlong era,and famous for coining mirror.Xue Family enjoyed a long history of making mirror, and the mirrors made by this family were of high quality and famous in Ming and Qing Dynasty. In Ming Wu Cheng County Chronicles,it is said "Hu Zhi Xue Jing Chi Ming.Xue,Hang Ren,Er Ye Yu Hu.Yi Mo Jing Bi Yong Hu Shui Wei Jia".Xue Huigong was the summit person of Xues in making mirror.

Looking through the 4,000-year development of Chinese bronze mirror,each era was marked its own features.From the small bronze mirrors,we can seemingly see the China's changes and transformations.Meanwhile,the bronze mirror,with special coinage,delicate patterns,strong artistic charming,are sparkling in China's civilization history.As time goes by,the bronze mirror fades away from our daily life,but its charm still exists in our heart.

图 版 PLATES

四山镜 战国

直径16.4厘米，边厚0.5厘米，重404克

1973年蚌埠市西郊八里桥出土

圆形。四弦钮，方钮座，外围凹面带方格。纹饰由地纹和主纹组合而成。地纹为羽状纹，地纹之上，于凹面方格的四角，向外延伸出四组连贯的花瓣，每组两瓣，在各组花瓣的顶端又连接一棒槌状的长叶纹，长叶纹均逆时针方向排列。四组花瓣和长叶纹将镜背分四区，每区置一左旋"山"字，"山"字笔画较瘦长。在各"山"字的右胁，装饰一片花瓣，全镜花瓣均以窄带纹相连接，共十二花瓣四长叶。素宽卷缘。

山字纹镜，是战国时期十分流行的镜类，一般按所饰山字的数量分三山、四山、五山和六山镜四种，其中又以四山镜居多。关于山字纹的起源，普遍认为是由青铜器上勾连云雷纹演变而来。此镜铸造精美，镜体轻巧，纹饰细密，山字自然灵动，是典型的楚式镜。

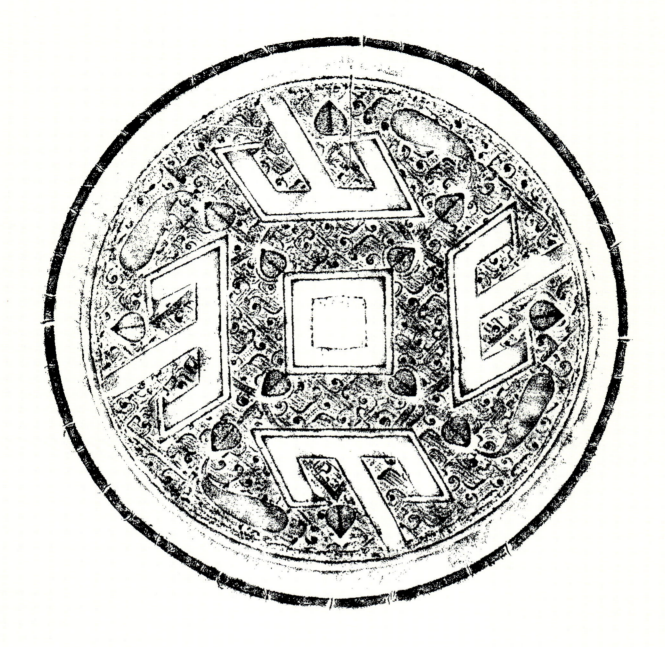

Mirror with inscription of four "Shan" characters Warring States Period

Diameter:16.4cm,Thickness of rim: 0.5cm,Weight:404gram

Unearthed at Bali Bridge,western suburbs of Bengbu City in 1973

The mirror is round in shape.It has a knob with four-string design on a square base,outside the base is adored with a concave surface square.The patterns on the mirror are formed by ground motif and main motif.The ground motif is decorated with feather-like pattern,on which there are four consistent groups of petal extend from the four corners of the concave surfaced square,each group has two pieces of petal,on the top of each petal connects with a wooden club shaped long-leaf pattern which arranged in anticlockwise.The back side of bronze mirror is divided into four regions by four groups of petal and long-leaf pattern,each region cast a left-handed and slender strokes "Shan" inscription.There is one piece of petal decorate on the right rib of each "Shan" ,there are 12 petals and 4 long-leaf in total,among which,all the petals are connected with narrow band pattern.The mirror has a broad rim showing no design and rolling.

Mirror with inscription of "Shan" characters prevailed very much among the populace during Waring State Period,usually classified as three,four,five and six"Shan"mirror according to the number of "Shan" characters,especially mirror with inscription of four "Shan"characters cast more.About the origin of "Shan" character pattern,it's generally thought that "Shan" is derived from thunder pattern on the bronzes. This mirror with delicate casting,thin and light mirror body,intricate and elegant decorations,natural and smart "Shan" characters,is a typical mirror of the the Chu State.

连弧纹日光镜　西汉

直径6.3厘米，边厚0.2厘米，重35克

蚌埠市博物馆旧藏

　　圆形。圆钮，圆钮座。座外围一周内向八连弧纹，钮座与连弧纹之间有几何纹组成简单的纹饰。其外两周栉齿纹之间有铭文圈带："见日之光，天下大明。"每字间隔以月牙纹和"◈"纹。素宽平缘。此镜字体较为特别，为篆隶式变体字，即从篆书向隶书转变的一种字体。

Mirror with linked arcs design and inscription of "Ri Gang"　Western Han Dynasty

Diameter:6.3cm,Thickness of the rim:0.2cm,Weight:35gram

Collected from Yangzhou City,Jiangsu Province

　　The mirror is round in shape.It has a round knob on a round base.Outside the base is a band of eight linked arcs inside.Between the base and linked arcs are patterns formed by simple geometries. Outside the pattern are two bands of fine-toothed pattern with a circle band of inscriptions inside:"Jian Ri Zhi Guang,Tian Xia Da Ming".The characters are spaced with crescent pattern and ◈-shaped pattern.The mirror has a broad and flat rim without design.The characters that cast on the mirror are very special,they are caved in form changing between seal and official scripts.

连弧纹日光镜 西汉

直径7.4厘米，边厚0.2厘米，重45克

蚌埠市博物馆旧藏

　　圆形。圆钮，圆钮座。座外围一周内向八连弧纹，钮座与连弧纹之间有几何纹组成简单的纹饰。其外两周栉齿纹之间有铭文一圈带："见日之光，天下大明。"每字间隔以"ⓔ"纹和"◈"纹。素宽平缘。

Mirror with linked arcs design and inscription of "Ri Gang" Western Han Dynasty

Diameter:7.4cm,Thickness of the rim:0.2cm,Weight:45gram

Collected from Yangzhou City,Jiangsu Province

　　The mirror is round in shape.It has a round knob on a round base.Outside the base is a band of eight linked arcs inside.Between the base and linked arcs are patterns formed by simple geometries. Outside the pattern are two bands of fine-toothed pattern with a circle band of inscriptions inside:"Jian Ri Zhi Guang,Tian Xia Da Ming".The characters are spaced with ⓔ-shaped pattern and ◈-shaped pattern. The mirror has a broad rim without design and has a flat surface.

连弧纹昭明镜　西汉
直径9.1厘米，缘厚0.5厘米，重172克
五河县征集

　　圆形。圆钮，圆钮座。座外围一周内向八连弧纹。其外两周栉齿纹之间有铭文圈带："内而青而以而昭而明，光而日月。"素宽平缘。此镜字体为篆隶式变体字，流行年代应稍早。昭明镜是汉代出土最多、流行范围最广的镜类之一，简洁质朴，以铭文作为装饰主题，对研究古代文字演变提供了重要史料。

Mirror with linked arcs design and inscription of "Zhao Ming"   Western Han Dynasty

Diameter:9.1cm,Thickness of the rim:0.5cm,Weight:172gram

Collected from Wuhe Country

The mirror is round in shape.It has a round knob on a round base.Outside the base is a band of eight linked arcs inside.Outside the pattern are two bands of fine-toothed patterns with a circle band of inscription inside:"Nei Yi Qing Er Yi Er Zhao Er Ming,Guang Er Ri Yue."The mirror has a broad rim without design and has a flat surface. The characters were caved in form changing between seal and official scripts and fashioned in early time.Mirror with inscription of "Zhao Ming" is one of bronze mirrors which were unearthed in the largest number and were popular the most widely in Han Dynasty,simple and rustic.This kind of mirror mainly decorated with inscription provides important historical information for studying ancient characters changing.

连弧纹昭明镜 西汉

直径10.3厘米，边厚0.4厘米，重218克

蚌埠市博物馆旧藏

　　圆形。圆钮，圆钮座。座外饰一周凸弦纹及内向八连弧　　月。"每两字之间夹一"而"字，铭文字体方正。素宽平缘。铭
纹。其外两周栉齿纹之间有铭文圈带："内清质以昭明，象夫日　　文中的"而"是一种间隔符号，并无实际意义。

Mirror with linked arcs design and inscription of "Zhao Ming" Western Han Dynasty

Diameter:10.3cm,Thickness of the rim:0.4cm,Weight:218gram

Collection of Bengbu Museum

The mirror is round in shape,it has a round knob on a round base. Outside the base is a circle band of raised string pattern and eight linked arcs inward.Then there are two bands of fine-toothed patterns with a circle band of inscription "Nei Qing Zhi Yi Zhao Ming,Xiang Fu Ri Yue" which is spaced with a Er character between each two words,the Er character has no actual meaning.The characters are in square upright form.The mirror has a broad rim without design and has a flat surface.

连弧纹昭明镜　西汉
直径10.5厘米，边厚0.5厘米，重210克
蚌埠市博物馆旧藏

　　圆形。圆钮，圆钮座。座外饰一周凸弦纹及内向十连弧纹。钮座与凸弦纹之间、凸弦纹与连弧纹之间有短线组成的简单纹饰。其外两周栉齿纹之间有铭文圈带："内清以昭明，光象夫日月，不泄。"每两字之间夹一"而"字，铭文字体方正。素宽平缘。

Mirror with linked arcs design and inscription of "Zhao Ming"   Western Han Dynasty

Diameter:10.5cm,Thickness of the rim:0.5cm,Weight:210gram

Collection of Bengbu Museum

The mirror is round in shape,it has a round knob on a round base. Outside the base is a circle band of raised string and ten linked arcs pattern inward.There are simple patterns formed by short lines adored in the space between the base and raided string,the raised string and linked arcs pattern.Outside that are two bands of fine-toothed pattern which spaced with inscription band "Nei Qing Yi Zhao Ming,Guang Xiang Fu Ri Yue, Bu Xie",each two words are spaced with a Er character which in square and upright form.The mirror has a broad rim without design and has a flat surface.

连弧纹昭明镜 西汉

直径8.9厘米，边厚0.4厘米，重168克

蚌埠市博物馆旧藏

　　圆形。圆钮，圆钮座。座外饰内向八连弧纹一周，钮座和连弧纹之间有短线组成的简单纹饰。其外两周栉齿纹之间有铭文圈带："内而清而以昭明，光而象夫日月，心而。"铭文字体较方正，但多简笔字，字句不完整。素宽平缘。

Mirror with linked arcs design and inscription of "Zhao Ming"   Western Han Dynasty

Diameter:8.9cm,Thickness of the rim:0.4cm,Weight:168gram

Collection of Bengbu Museum

The mirror is round in shape,it has a round knob on a round base.Outside the base is a circle band of eight linked arcs pattern inward,there are simple designs formed by short lines between the base and linked arcs pattern.Outside that are two circle bands of fine-toothed pattern with inscription spaced with: "Nei Er Qing Yi Zhao Ming,Guang Er Xiang Fu Ri Yue,Xin Er",the characters are in square and upright font,but mostly are short one with incomplete sentence.The mirror has a broad rim without design and has a flat surface.

连弧纹昭明镜　西汉

直径8厘米，边厚0.35厘米，重118克
蚌埠市博物馆旧藏

　　圆形。圆钮，圆钮座。座外饰内向十二弧纹一周。其外两周栉齿纹之间有铭文圈带："内清以昭明，光日月。"每两字之间夹一"而"字，铭文字体方正。素宽平缘。

Mirror with linked arcs design and inscription of "Zhao Ming"　Western Han Dynasty

Diameter:8cm,Thickness of the rim:0.35cm,Weight:118gram
Collection of Bengbu Museum

　　The mirror is round in shape,it has a round knob on a round base. Outside the base is a band of twelve linked arcs pattern inward.Out of that are two bands of fine-toothed pattern which spaced with a band of inscription: "Nei Qing Yi Zhao Ming,Guang Ri Yue",each two words spaced with a Er character.The inscriptions are in square and upright font.The mirror has a broad rim without design and has a flat surface.

连弧纹昭明镜　西汉

直径9厘米，边厚0.55厘米，重183克
1984年固镇县城关镇张识大队朱之强先生送交

圆形。圆钮，圆钮座。座外围一周内向八连弧纹，钮座与连弧纹之间有短线组成简单的纹饰。其外两周栉齿纹之间有铭文圈带："内清而以昭明，光而象夫日之月，心忽而不泄。"素宽平缘。

Mirror with linked arcs design and inscription of "Zhao Ming"　Western Han Dynasty

Diameter:9cm,Thickness of the rim:0.55cm,Weight:183gram
Donated by Mr Zhu Zhiqiang from Zhangshi Team,Guzhen Country in 1984

The mirror is round in shape,it has a round knob on a round base. Outside the base is a band of eight linked arcs pattern inward.There are simple patterns formed by short lines between the base and linked arcs pattern.There is a band of inscription: "Nei Qing Er Yi Zhao Ming,Guang Er Xiang Fu Ri Zhi Yue,Xin Hu Er Bu Xie."Both sides of the inscription are adored with a band of fine-toothed pattern.The mirror has a broad rim without design and has a flat surface.

连弧纹昭明镜　西汉

直径8.4厘米,边厚0.45厘米，重110克
2001年蚌埠市铁路派出所查获移交

　　圆形。圆钮，圆钮座。座外围一周内向十二连弧纹，钮座与　　圈带："内而清而质以而昭而明，光而象日而月。"素宽平缘。
连弧纹之间有短线组成简单的纹饰。其外两周栉齿纹之间有铭文

Mirror with linked arcs design and inscription of "Zhao Ming"　Western Han Dynasty

Diameter:8.4cm,Thickness of the rim:0.45cm,Weight:110gram

Seized and transferred by Railway Station Public Security in Bengbu City in 2001

　　The mirror is round in shape,it has a round knob on a round base.Outside the base is a band of twelve linked arcs pattern inward. There are simple patterns formed by short lines between the base and linked arcs pattern.There is a band of inscription: "Nei Er Qing Er Zhi Er Yi Er Zhao Er Ming,Guang Er Xiang Ri Er Yue."Both sides of the inscription are adored with a band of fine-toothed pattern.The mirror has a broad rim without design and has a flat surface.

四乳四螭镜 西汉
直径8.2厘米，边厚0.4厘米，重100克
蚌埠市博物馆旧藏

圆形。圆钮，圆钮座。座外围一周凸弦纹。钮座与凸弦纹之间有短线组成的简单纹饰。其外两周带齿纹之间，等距离的分布着四枚圆座乳钉纹，空白处填以四螭。四螭成钩形躯体，两端同形，螭的身躯外侧各填饰一只禽鸟纹。素宽平缘。

螭，形似小蛇，是古代传说中著名的山林鬼物，其原型来自是蜥蜴，被认为是图案稍简化的龙的形象。《述异记》载："螭五百年化为蛟，蛟千年化为龙。"

Mirror with design of four nipples and four serpents Western Han Dynasty
Diameter:8.2cm,Thickness of the rim:0.4cm,Weight:100gram
Collection of Bengbu Museum

The mirror is round in shape,it has a round knob on a round base. Outside the base is a band of raised string.Between the base and the raised string are simple patterns formed by short lines.Outside that are two bands of fine-toothed pattern which distribute equidistantly design of four nipples with round base,in the spaced adored with four hook-shaped serpents which has same style on both side.Each body side of the serpent decorated with a bird.The mirror has a broad rim without design and has a flat surface.

Serpent is the famous creature live in mountains in ancient legend which has a snake body comes from the lizard image,considered to be a simplified pattern of the image of dragon.The Note Record Strange says,A serpent takes five hundreds years to change into a Jiao,a Jiao needs one thousand years to change into a dragon.

四乳四虺镜 西汉

直径9.8厘米，边厚0.4厘米，重173克

蚌埠市博物馆旧藏

　　圆形。圆钮，圆钮座。座外围一周宽面凸弦纹。钮座与凸弦纹之间有短线组成的简单纹饰。其外两周栉齿纹之间，等距离分布着四枚圆座乳钉纹，空白处填以四虺，四虺成钩形躯体，两端同形，虺的身躯外侧各填饰一只禽鸟纹。素宽平缘。

Mirror with design of four nipples and four serpents Western Han Dynasty   Western Han Dynasty

Diameter:9.8cm,Thickness of the rim:0.4cm,Weight:173gram

Collection of Bengbu Museum

The mirror is round in shape,it has a round knob on a round base. Outside the base is a broad band of raised string.Between the base and the raised string are simple patterns formed by short lines.Outside that are two bands of fine-toothed pattern which distribute equidistantly design of four nipples with round base,in the spaced adored with four hook-shaped serpents which has same style on both side.Each body side of the serpent decorated with a bird.The mirror has a broad rim without design and has a flat surface.

四乳四虺镜 西汉
直径10.3厘米，边厚0.35厘米，重225克
1990年天河乡供销社汉墓出土

　　圆形。圆钮，圆钮座。座外围一周凸弦纹。钮座与凸弦纹之间有短线组成的简单纹饰。其外两周栉齿纹之间，等距离分布着四枚圆座乳钉纹，空白处填以四虺，四虺成钩形躯体，两端同形，虺的身躯两侧各填饰一只禽鸟纹。素宽平缘。

Mirror with design of four nipples and four serpents   Western Han Dynasty

Diameter:10.3cm,Thickness of the rim:0.35cm,Weight:225gram
Unearthed at Han Tomb in Tianhe Commune in 1990

The mirror is round in shape,it has a round knob on a round base. Outside the base is a band of raised string.Between the base and the raised string are simple patterns formed by short lines.Outside that are two bands of fine-toothed pattern which distribute equidistantly design of four nipples with round base,in the spaced adored with four hook-shaped serpents which has same style on both side.Each body side of the serpent decorated with a bird.The mirror has a broad rim without design and has a flat surface.

四乳禽兽镜 西汉

直径13.5厘米，边厚0.4厘米，重374克

2001年邰常来先生捐赠

圆形。圆钮，柿蒂纹钮座。座外围栉齿纹和宽平凸弦纹圈带各一周。其外两周栉齿纹间，等距离分布着四枚圆座乳钉，四乳将镜背分四区，分别填饰白虎、朱雀和禽兽。白虎作行走状，朱雀作飞翔状。一走兽作奔跑状，另一走兽作伫立回首状，细线条勾勒，生动形象。素宽平缘。

Mirror with design of four nipples and animals Western Han Dynasty

Diameter:13.5cm,Thickness of the rim:0.4cm,Weight:374gram

Collected from Mr Tai Changlai in 2001

The mirror is round in shape,it has a round knob on a base with kaki calyx design.Outside the base are a band of fine-toothed pattern and a broad band of raised string.Then out these designs are two bands of fine-toothed pattern with which distribute equidistantly design of four nipples with round base,the four nipples divided the mirror into four sections spaced with a moving White Tiger,a flying Scarlet Bird,two beasts which one is running and the other is standing and turning around.The vivid animals are cast with thin lines.The mirror has a broad rim without design and has a flat surface.

连弧纹昭明镜 东汉

直径12.9厘米，边厚0.65厘米，重415克

蚌埠市博物馆旧藏

　　圆形。圆钮，并蒂十二连珠纹钮座。座外饰一周宽平凸弦纹及内向八连弧纹。其外两周栉齿纹之间有铭文圈带："内而清而以昭明，光而象夫而日之月，而心忽而忠而不泄 。"素宽平缘。

此镜尺寸较大，铸制精美，纹饰清晰，与西汉时期简洁质朴的风格不同，流行年代应该稍晚。

Mirror with linked arcs design and inscription of "Zhao Ming" Eastern Han Dynasty

Diameter:12.9cm,Thickness of the rim:0.65cm,Weight:415gram

Collection of Bengbu Museum

The mirror is round in shape,it has a round knob on a base with design of double pedicels of twelve peals.Outside the base is a band of broad and flat raised string pattern and eight linked arcs pattern inward. There is a band of inscription: "Nei Er Qing Er Yi Zhao Ming,Guang Er Xiang Fu Ri Yue,Er Xin Hu Er Zhong Er Bu Xie."Both sides of the inscription are adored with a band of fine-toothed pattern.The rim showing no design is broad and has a flat surface.It has a big size with delicate mold and clear pattern,different from the simple and rustic style of the Western Han Dynasty and popular in the late time.

日有熹铭连弧纹镜　东汉

直径15.1厘米，边厚0.7厘米，重725克

1983年怀远县龙亢向桥公社砖室墓出土

　　圆形。圆钮，柿蒂纹钮座。座外饰一周凸弦纹及内向八连弧　　熹，月有富，乐无事，宜酒食，居必安，无患忧，竽瑟侍，心志
纹，间饰叶芽状纹饰。其外两周栉齿纹之间有铭文圈带："日有　　欢，乐已茂，固常"。素宽平缘。

Mirror with linked arcs design and inscription of "Ri You Xi"   Eastern Han Dynasty

Diameter:15.1cm,Thickness of the rim:0.7cm,Weight:725gram

Unearthed at a tile tomb,Long Gang Town,Xiang Bridge Commune in Bengbu City in1983

The mirror is round in shape,it has a round knob on a base with kaki calyx design.Outside the base is a band of raised string pattern and eight linked arcs pattern inward which spaced with leaf-bud-shaped design.There is a band of inscription: "Ri You Xi,Yue You Fu,Le Wu Shi,Yi Jiu Shi,Ju Bi An,Wu You Huan,Yu Se Shi,Xin Zhi Huan,Yue Yi Mao,Gu Chang."Both sides of the inscription are adored with a band of fine-toothed pattern.The mirror has a broad rim without design and has a flat surface.

四乳禽兽镜 东汉
直径11.1厘米，边厚0.7厘米，重315克
蚌埠市博物馆旧藏

　　圆形。圆钮，圆钮座。座外等距离分布四枚圆座乳钉纹，乳
钉纹将镜背分四区，四区内填饰白虎、羽人、走兽和飞禽。白虎
作奔跑状，羽人作蹲坐回首状，禽兽作攀援状，禽鸟作伫立回首
状，空白处填以简单的几何纹作装饰。外围一周栉齿纹。宽缘，
缘上饰锯齿纹和双线波折纹各一周。此镜刻画清晰，造型生动，
栩栩如生，极富动感。

Mirror with design of four deities and gambling   Eastern Han Dynasty

Diameter:11.1cm,Thickness of the rim:0.7cm,Weight:315gram

Collection of Bengbu Museum

The mirror is round in shape,it has a round knob on a round base.Outside the base distribute equidistantly four nipples with round base which divided the mirror into four sections adored with White Tiger,winged figure,moving beasts and flying birds,among that the White Tiger is running,the winged figure is sitting and turning around,the beasts are climbing,the birds are standing and turning around.While in the space of the pattern decorated with simple geometry pattern.Outside is a band of fine-toothed pattern.On the broad rim has saw pattern and wave pattern formed with double lines.The mirror is cast clearly with vivid modeling and full of innervation.

四乳四凤镜 东汉

直径10厘米、边厚0.4厘米、重188克
蚌埠市博物馆旧藏

　　圆形。圆钮，圆钮座。座外环一周凸弦纹，其间填饰8组三条短线组成的简单纹饰。其外两周栉齿纹之间等距离分布着四枚圆座乳钉，四乳将镜背分四区，每区填饰一只凤鸟，四凤形态一致，皆昂首、振翅、尾翼卷起，作冲天状。宽缘，缘上饰双线波折纹一周。

Mirror with design of four nipples and four phoenixes Eastern Han Dynasty

Diameter:10cm,Thickness of the rim:0.4cm,Weight:188gram

Collection of Bengbu Museum

The mirror is round in shape,it has a round knob on a round base. Outside the base is a band of raised string pattern which spaced with eight groups of simple pattern formed by three short lines.Outside that distribute equidistant four nipples with round base between the two bands of fine-toothed pattern.The four nipples divide the back side of the bronze mirror into four zones with a phoenix in each zone. The four phoenixes are in same shape flying into the sky with heads raising,wings opening and tails rolling up.On the broad rim has a band a wave pattern formed with double lines.

蚌埠市博物馆
铜镜集萃

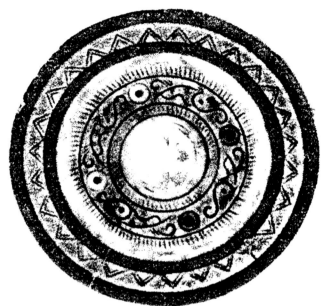

四乳禽鸟镜 东汉

直径8.2厘米，边厚0.2厘米，重84克

1985年固镇县出土

圆形。圆钮，圆钮座。座外环一周凸弦纹，其间填饰4组两条短线组成的简单纹饰。其外两周栉齿纹之间等距离分布着四枚圆座乳钉，四乳将镜背分四区，每区填饰一只凤鸟，四凤形态一致，皆昂首，振翅，尾翼卷起，作冲天状。宽缘，缘上饰双线波折纹一周。

Mirror with design of four nipples and birds　Eastern Han Dynasty

Diameter:8.2cm,Thickness of the rim:0.2cm,Weight:84gram

Unearthed at Guzhen Country in 1985

The mirror is round in shape,it has a round knob on a round base.Outside the base is a band of raised string pattern which spaced with four groups of simple patterns formed by two short lines.Outside that distribute equidistant four nipples with round base between the two bands of fine-toothed pattern.The four nipples divide the back side of the bronze mirror into four zones with a phoenix in each zone. The four phoenixes are in same shape flying into the sky with heads raising,wings opening and tails rolling up.On the broad rim has a band a wave pattern formed with double lines.

四乳八禽镜　东汉
直径8.5厘米，边厚0.4厘米，重110克
蚌埠市博物馆旧藏

　　圆形。圆钮，柿蒂纹钮座。座外围双线凹面方框一周。方框外四边中点处置着四枚圆座乳钉纹，四乳两侧各饰一禽鸟，隔乳相背而立。其外围一周栉齿纹。凸缘，缘上饰一周单线波折纹。

Mirror with design of four nipples and eight birds　Eastern Han Dynasty
Diameter:8.5cm,Thickness of the rim:0.4cm,Weight:110gram
Collection of Bengbu Museum

　　The mirror is round in shape,it has a round knob on a base with kaki calyx design.Outside the base is a square with concave surface formed by double lines,outside the square distribute four nipples with round base at the middle point of the four lines of the square,each sides of the nipples decorate with a bird and standing back to back separated by the nipple.Outside that is a band of fine-toothed pattern.On the raised rim is a band of wave pattern formed by single line.

四神博局镜 东汉
直径10厘米，边厚0.35厘米，重195克
蚌埠市博物馆旧藏

　　圆形。圆钮，柿蒂纹钮座。座外围双线凹面方框一周。其外饰"T、L、V"形博局纹，博局纹将镜背分成四方八区，空白处填以青龙、白虎、朱雀、玄武四神兽，各据一方，每神又配一只禽兽，隔"V"形纹相对而立。外围一周栉齿纹。宽缘，缘上饰双线波折纹，每一波折间填饰一点珠纹。

　　四神，也叫作四象，是中国古代神话中的四方之神灵，即东方青龙、西方白虎、南方朱雀、北方玄武（多为龟蛇合体）。春秋战国时期，由于五行学说盛行，所以四象也被配色成为青龙、白虎、朱雀、玄武。两汉时期，四象演化成为道教所信奉的神灵，故而四象也随即被称为四灵，并被赋予了"镇四方，避不祥"的守护神职能，作为一种祥瑞纹饰在汉镜上广泛出现。

Mirror with design of four deities and gambling   Eastern Han Dynasty

Diameter:8.5cm,Thickness of the rim:0.4cm,Weight:110gram

Collection of Bengbu Museum

The mirror is round in shape.It has a round knob on a base with kaki calyx design.Outside is a with concave surface square formed by double lines.Outside the square decorate with T.L.V-shaped gambling design which divide the mirror into four zones,in the space adored with four deities of Green Dragon,White Tiger,Scarlet Bird and Somber Warrior arranged the four corners,each deity adored with a mythical beast standing face to face separated by the "V"character.Outside the major motif is adored with a band of fine-toothed pattern.The mirror has a broad rim.On the rim has a band of wave pattern formed by double lines,each wave spaced with a little pearl design.

The four deities are also called the four images,known as the four gods protect the four positions in ancient mythology,the Green Dragon in the East,the White Tiger in the West,the Scarlet Bird in the South,the Somber Warrior in the North(the Somber Warrior is a combination of tortoise and snake).The four images are described and colored as Green Dragon,White Tiger,Scarlet Bird and Somber Warrior because of the prevail of Five Element Theory during the Spring and Autumn Period and the Warring State.When the two Han Dynasties,the four images evolved into the gods which believed by Taoism,so they are also called the Four Deities and given the function of protect and avoid the ominous things,as a kind of auspicious patterns widely appeared on the Han mirror.

尚方铭八乳四神博局镜　东汉

直径17.8厘米，边厚0.5厘米，重798克

2009年蚌埠市禹会区九龙集万隆汽配场墓葬群M8出土

　　圆形。圆钮，柿蒂纹钮座。座外饰凸弦纹方框和双线凹面方框各一周。其间十二枚圆座乳钉和十二地支铭文绕钮相间列列。凹面方框外环列八枚圆座乳钉纹和四组"T、L、V"形博局纹，乳钉纹和博局纹将镜背分成四方八区，空白处填饰青龙、白虎、朱雀、玄武四神，各据一方，每神配一只禽兽作装饰，隔"V"纹相对而立。其外一周铭文圈带："尚方作竟真大巧，上有仙人不知老，渴饮玉泉饥食枣，浮游天下敖四海。"外围一周栉齿纹。宽缘，缘上饰两周锯齿纹和一周双线波折纹。

　　"尚方"是汉代为皇室制作御用物品的官署，属少府。尚方铭镜为御制镜，质量上乘，纹饰精美。当时，民间有很多工匠假借尚方制镜的名义作镜，相比而言，质量粗糙。

Mirror with inscription of "Shang Fang" and design of eight nipples,four deities and gambling Eastern Han Dynasty

Diameter:17.8cm,Thickness of the rim:0.5cm,Weight:798gram

Unearthed at Tombs M8 of Wanlong Auto Parts Factory in Kowloon Town,Yuhui District,Bengbu City in 2009

The mirror is round in shape.It has a round knob on a base with kaki calyx design.Outside the base are two squares,one is formed by raising string pattern,the other one is formed by double lines concave surface.Between the squares there are design of twelve nipples with round base and inscription of twelve Earthly Branches interphase around the knob.Outside the concave surface square are eight nipples with round base and four groups of "T.L.V"gambling design which divided the mirror into four zones,each corner of the square decorated with Green Dragon,White Tiger,Scarlet Bird and Somber Warrior,while each deity adored with a mythical beast,the deity and the mythical beast standing face to face separated by a "V"design.Outside that is a band of inscription "Shang Fang Zuo Jing Zhen Da Qiao,Shang You Xian Ren Bu Zhi Lao,Ke Yin Yu Quan Ji Shi Zao,Fu You Tian Xia Ao Si Hai".Outside the major motif adored a band of fine-toothed pattern.The broad rim is adored with two bands of saw pattern and a band of wave pattern formed by double lines.

"Shang Fang"was the department that made production only used for Royal in Han Dynasty which under the charge of department named "Shao Fu".Royal-made mirror was used only by royalty with high quality and exquisite pattern.At that time,there were many civil craftsmen made false mirror with rough technology under the name of Royal-made.

尚方铭八乳四神博局镜 东汉

直径20厘米，边厚0.3厘米，重817克

蚌埠市博物馆旧藏

　　圆形。圆钮，柿蒂纹钮座。座外围双线凹面方框一周。钮座与方框间十二枚圆座小乳钉和十二地支铭文相间环列。其外分布八枚圆座乳钉纹和"T、L、V"博局纹，乳钉纹和博局纹将镜背分成四方八区，空白处填饰青龙、白虎、朱雀、玄武四神，各据一方，每神配一只禽兽作装饰，隔"V"纹相对而立。其外一周铭文圈带："尚方作竟真大巧，上有仙人不知老，渴饮玉泉饥食枣，浮游天下□□□，寿如金石□。"宽缘，缘上饰两周锯齿纹和一周波折纹。

Mirror with inscription of "Shang Fang"and design of eight nipples,four deities and gambling　Eastern Han Dynasty

Diameter:20cm,Thickness of rim:0.3cm,Weight:817gram

Collected from Hero Mountain Market,Jinan,Shandong Province in 1996

The mirror is round in shape.It has a round knob on a base with kaki calyx design.Outside the base adored with a concave surface square formed by double lines.Between the base and square are twelve small nipples with round base and inscription of twelve Earthly Branches alternately arranged.Outside that are eight nipples with round base and T.L.V-shaped gambling design which divided the mirror into four zones,each corner of the square decorated with Green Dragon,White Tiger,Scarlet Bird and Somber Warrior,while each deity adored with a mythical beast,the deity and the mythical beast standing face to face separated by a "V"design.Outside that is a band of inscription "Shang Fang Zuo Jing Zhen Da Qiao,Shang You Xian Ren Bu Zhi Lao,Ke Yin Yu Quan Ji Shi Zao,Fu You Tian Xia□□□,Shou Ru Jin Shi□".The broad rim is adored with two bands of saw pattern and a band of wave pattern.

长宜子孙铭八乳四神博局镜　东汉

直径14.4厘米，边厚0.45厘米，重484克
蚌埠市博物馆旧藏

　　圆钮，柿蒂纹钮座，其间饰有"长宜子孙"四字。座外饰双线凹面方框一周。其外饰"T、L、V"形博局纹，博局纹将镜背分成四方八区，空白处填以青龙、白虎、朱雀、玄武、禽鸟和禽兽等。外围一周铭文："□□之纪从竟（镜）始，长葆二亲利孙子，辟去不羊（祥）宜古（贾）市，寿如石，西王母□□□往乐乃□。"一周栉齿纹为廓。宽缘，缘上饰锯齿纹和云气纹。

Mirror with inscription of "Chang Yi Zi Sun" and design of eight nipples, four deities and gambling　Eastern Han Dynasty

Diameter:14.4cm,Thickness of rim:0.45cm,Weight:484gram
Collection of Bengbu Museum

　　The mirror has a round knob and a base with kaki calyx design with four inscriptions of "Chang Yi Zi Sun" alternated arranged.Outside the base is a concave surface square formed by double lines.Outside the square is adored with T.L.V-shaped gambling design which divied the mirror into four zones.Each zone spaced with animals design including Green Dragon,White Tiger,Scarlet Bird,Somber Warrior,birds,beasts and so on.Outside that is a band of inscription: "□□Zhi Ji Cong Jing Shi,Chang Bao Er Qin Li Sun Zi,Bi Qu Bu Xiang Yi Gu Shi,Shou Ru Shi,Xi Wang Mu□□□Wang Le Nai□."Outside the major motif adored a band of fine-toothed pattern.The broad rim is adored with saw patterns and cloud designs.

君宜官秩铭禽兽纹博局镜 东汉
直径12.3厘米，边厚0.4厘米，重340克
蚌埠市博物馆旧藏

圆形。圆钮，圆钮座。钮与钮座间有短线组成简单的纹饰。座外围双线凹面方框一周，方框的内四角逆时针分布着四字铭文"君宜官秩"。方框外环列八枚圆座乳钉纹和四组"T、L、V"形博局纹，乳钉纹和博局纹将镜背分成四方八区，空白处填以青龙、白虎、玄武、禽兽和禽鸟作装饰，隔"V"纹相对而立。其外一周铭文圈带："柰言之始自有纪，涷冶铜锡去其宰，辟除不详宜古市，长葆二亲利子孙。"外饰栉齿纹一周。宽缘，缘上饰锯齿纹和云气纹。

Mirror with inscriptions of "Shang Fang"and design of eight nipples,eight birds and gambling   Eastern Han Dynasty
Diameter:12.3cm,Thickness of rim:0.4cm,Weight:340gram
Collection of Bengbu Museum

The mirror is round in shape.It has a round knob on a round base.Between the knob and base are simple pattern formed by short lines.Outside the base is a concave surface square formed by double lines.On the corners of the square are four inscriptions of Jun Yi Guan Zhi arranged in an anticlockwise direction.Outside the square are eight nipples with round base and four groups of T.L.V gambling design which divide the mirror into four zones decorated with Green Dragon,White Tiger,Somber Warrior,birds and beasts.The patterns are standing face to face separated by a V-shaped pattern.Outside the major motif is a band of inscription: "Shu Yan Zhi Shi Zi You Ji,Jian Zhi Tong Qu Qi Zai,Bi Chu Bu Xiang Yi Gu Shi,Chang Bao Er Qin Yi Zi Sun."Outside the inscription is adored with a band of fine-toothed pattern.The broad rim is adored with saw pattern and cloud pattern.

禽兽纹博局镜 东汉

直径9.9厘米，边厚0.3厘米，重137克

蚌埠市博物馆旧藏

　　圆形。圆钮，柿蒂纹钮座。座外饰"T、L、V"形博局纹，博局纹将镜背分成四方八区，空白处填以青龙、白虎、玄武和禽　　兽。其中青龙、白虎独占一方，玄武配蛇，另一方为双禽。外围一周栉齿纹。宽缘，缘上饰双线波折纹一周。

Mirror with design of animal and gambling Eastern Han Dynasty

Diameter:9.9cm,Thickness of rim:0.3cm,Weight:137gram

Collection of Bengbu Museum

The mirror is round in shape.It has a round knob on a base with kaki calyx design.Outside the base are adored with T.L.V-shaped gambling designs which divide the mirror into four zones.The major motif is spaced with patterns of Green Dragon,White Tiger,Somber Warrior,birds and beasts.Among that,the Green Dragon and White Tiger occupy a single part of the square separately,the Somber Warrior adored with a snake and the other part are two birds.Outside the major motif adored a band of fine-toothed pattern.The broad rim is adored with a band of wave pattern formed by double lines.

尚方铭八乳八禽博局镜 东汉
直径13厘米，边厚0.5厘米，重289克
蚌埠市博物馆旧藏

　　圆形。圆钮，四叶纹钮座。座外围双线凹面方框一周。方框外环列八乳钉和四组"T、L、V"形博局纹，乳钉纹和博局纹将镜背分成四方八区，空白处填以八只禽鸟和简单的几何纹，每组博局纹之间的两只禽鸟相背而立，隔V纹两两相对。其外一周铭文圈带："尚方作竟真大好，上有山人不（知）老，渴饮玉泉。"外饰栉齿纹一周。宽缘，缘上饰锯齿纹和云气纹各一周。

Mirror with inscriptions of "Shang Fang"and design of eight nipples,eight birds and gambling   Eastern Han Dynasty

Diameter:13cm,Thickness of rim:0.5cm,Weight:289gram

Collection of Bengbu Museum

The mirror is round in shape.It has a round knob on a base with four-leaves design.Outside the base is a concave surface square formed by double lines.Outside the square decorate with eight nipples and four groups of T.L.V gambling designs which divide the mirror into four zones with decoration of eight birds and simple geometry pattern.Each group of two birds cast between the gambling design standing back to back separate by the V pattern.Outside that is a band of inscription: "Shang Fang Zuo Jing Zhen Da Hao,Shang You Shan Ren Bu (Zhi) Lao,KeYin Yu Quan."Outside the inscription is adored with a band of fine-toothed pattern.The broad rim is adored with saw pattern and cloud pattern.

八乳几何纹博局镜 东汉

直径12厘米，边厚0.45厘米，重364克
蚌埠市博物馆旧藏

　　圆形。圆钮，柿蒂纹钮座。座外围双线凹面方框一周。其外　　纹做装饰，外围一周栉齿纹。宽缘，缘上饰两周锯齿纹。此镜纹
等距离分布八枚圆座乳钉纹和"T、L、V"博局纹，空白处填以钩　　饰简洁，短线勾勒的图案，显得生动明快，别具一番韵味。

Mirror with design of eight nipples,geometry and gambling Eastern Han Dynasty

Diameter:12cm,Thickness of Rim:0.45,Weight:364gram

Collection of Bengbu Museum

The mirror is round in shape.It has a round knob on a base with kaki calyx design.Outside the base is a concave surface square formed by double lines,outside the square distribute eight nipples with round base and T.L.V-shaped gambling design in equal distance.In the space decorate with hook pattern.outside the major motif is a band of fine-toothed pattern.On the broad rim decorate with two bands of saw pattern.The mirror decorate with clean and simple design,pictures formed by short lines,which bring a vivid and bright effect and charm.

禽兽纹简化博局镜　东汉

直径10.2厘米，边厚0.3厘米，重192克

蚌埠市博物馆馆旧藏

　　圆形。圆钮，圆钮座。座外饰双线凹面方框一周。其外饰"T、V"形简化博局纹，博局纹将镜背分四区，每区填饰一神兽做装饰，一龙一虎双凤，龙虎相对排列，皆作行走态，双凤相对排列，皆展翅飞翔，外围一周栉齿纹。宽缘，缘上饰一周双线波折纹。

Mirror with design of animal and simple gambling Eastern Han Dynasty

Diameter:10.2cm,Thickness of Rim:0.3cm,Weight:192gram

Collection of Bengbu Museum

The mirror is round in shape.It has a round knob on a round base. Outside the base is a concave surface square formed by double lines. Outside the square adored with T.V-shaped simple gambling design which divide the mirror into four zones,each zone is spaced with a mythical beast,one dragon,one tiger and two phoenixes.Dragon and tiger were moving and arranged face to face,while the two phoenixes are fling and also arranged face to face.Outside the major motif is a band of fine-toothed pattern.On the broad rim decorate with a band of wave pattern formed by double lines.

禽兽纹简化博局镜 东汉

直径10厘米，边厚0.4厘米，重199克

蚌埠市博物馆旧藏

　　圆形。圆钮，圆钮座。座外环凸弦纹一周，其间填饰简单的几何纹和一周短线纹。其外分布"V"形简化博局纹，博局纹将镜背分四区，分别填饰羽人、朱雀和两只禽兽。羽人作行走状，朱雀作飞翔状，一只禽兽作伫立回首状，另一只作昂首翘尾状。细线勾勒，形象生动。宽缘，缘上饰单线波折纹一周，每一波折间填饰一点珠纹。

Mirror with design of animal and simple gambling   Eastern Han Dynasty

Diameter:10cm,Thickness of Rim:0.4cm,Weight:199gram

Collection of Bengbu Museum

The mirror is round in shape.It has a round knob on a round base.Outside the base is a band of raised string which spaced with simple geometry pattern and a band of short lines pattern.Outside that distribute V-shaped simple gambling designs which divide the mirror into four zones,each zone decorate with winged man,Scarlet Bird and two beasts.The winged man was moving,the Scarlet Bird was fling,one beast was standing still and turning around,the other beast was raising its head and tail.The mirror with thin line shows a vivid shape.On the broad rim decorate with a band of wave pattern formed by single line,each wave adored with a point of bead pattern.

作佳镜铭八乳简化博局镜　东汉
直径12厘米，边厚0.4厘米，重360克
蚌埠市博物馆旧藏

　　圆形。圆钮，圆钮座。座外围双线凹面方框一周。钮座与方框的内四角有四条短线相连，短线两侧置两点珠纹。方框外饰八枚圆座乳钉纹和四组"T"形简化博局纹，空白处填饰"◈"形几何纹符号。其外是一周铭文圈带："作佳镜□真大好，上有山人不知老，渴饮澧泉，饥"。外围栉齿纹一周。宽缘，缘上饰锯齿纹和云气纹。

Mirror with inscription of "zuo jia jing" and design of eight nipples and simple gambling Eastern Han Dynasty

Diameter:12cm,Thickness of Rim:0.4cm,Weight:360gram

Collection of Bengbu Museum

The mirror is round in shape.It has a round knob on a round base. Outside the base is a concave surface square formed by double lines. There are four short lines connect with the knob and the four corners of the square,both sides of the short lines adored with two points of bead pattern.Outside the square is decorate with eight nipples with round base and four groups of T-shaped simple gambling design which spaced with ◈-shaped geometry pattern.Outside that is a band of inscription: "Zuo Jia Jing□Zhen Da Hao,Shang You Shan Ren Bu Zhi Lao,Ke Yin Li Quan,Ji" which is surrounded with a band of fine-toothed pattern. The broad rim is decorated with saw pattern and cloud pattern.

几何纹简化博局镜　东汉

直径7.9厘米，边厚0.35厘米，重100克

蚌埠市博物馆旧藏

　　圆形。圆钮，圆钮座。座外围双线凹面方框一周。钮座向方框的内四角射出四条短线。方框外饰"T"形简化博局纹，空白处填饰"℮"形和短线形几何纹符号。外围栉齿纹一周。宽缘，缘上装饰锯齿纹，锯齿纹密布挺拔，犹如日之光辉，照耀大地。

Mirror with design of geometry and simple gambling　Eastern Han Dynasty

Diameter:7.9cm,Thickness of Rim:0.35cm,Weight:100gram

Collection of Bengbu Museum

　　The mirror is round in shape.It has a round knob on a round base. Outside the base is a concave surface square formed by double lines. There are four short lines connect with the knob and the four corners of the square.Outside the square is adored with T-shaped simple gambling design with ℮-shaped patterns and short-line-shaped geometry symbols in the space which is surrounded a band of fine-toothed pattern.The broad rim is decorated with lots of saw patterns which has tall and straight shapes,like sunshine.

几何纹简化博局镜 东汉

直径9厘米，边厚0.45厘米，重118克

蚌埠市博物馆旧藏

圆形。圆钮，圆钮座。座外围双线凹面圈带一周。其外分布四枚圆座乳钉纹和"T"形简化博局纹，空白处填饰几何纹。其外围栉齿纹一周。宽缘，缘上饰锯齿纹一周。此镜纹饰较为特别，短线勾绘的图案，好似一朵朵绽放的花苞，生机盎然。

Mirror with design of geometry and simple gambling Eastern Han Dynasty

Diameter:9cm,Thickness of Rim:0.45cm,Weight:118gram

Transferred by Mr Zheng Huaihe from the Electrical Engineering Team in Bengbu Railway Station

The mirror is round in shape.It has a round knob on a round base. Outside the base is a concave surface band formed by double lines.On the outer place decorate with patterns of four nipple with round base and T-shaped simple gambling design which adored with geometry pattern in the space.Outside the major motif is a band of fine-toothed pattern.The broad rim is adored with a band of saw pattern.The mirror with special bud-shaped pattern drew by short lines is brimming over with vigor and vitality.

新有善铜铭八乳几何纹简化博局镜 东汉

直径12厘米，边厚0.45厘米，重300克

蚌埠市博物馆旧藏

　　圆形。圆钮，圆钮座。座外围双线凹面方框一周。其外分布八枚圆座乳钉纹和"T、V"形简化博局纹，空白处填饰几何纹。外饰铭文圈带"新有善铜出丹阳，和以银锡清且明"。外围栉齿纹一周。宽缘，缘上饰卷云纹一周。

Mirror with inscription of "Xin You Shan Tong" and design of eight nipples,geometry and simple gambling   Eastern Han Dynasty

Diameter:12cm,Thickness of Rim:0.45cm,Weight:300gram

Collection of Bengbu Museum

    The mirror is round in shape.It has a round knob on a round base. Outside the base is a concave surface square formed by double lines. Outside the square is decorate with eight nipples with round base and four groups of T.V-shaped simple gambling design which spaced with geometry pattern.Outside the major motif is a band of inscription "Xin You Shan Tong Chu Dan Yan,He Yi Yin Xi Qing Qie Ming" which is surrounded with a band of fine-toothed pattern.The mirror has a broad rim with decoration of a band of rolling cloud pattern on it.

上大山见神人铭七乳神兽镜　东汉

直径15.5厘米，边厚0.5厘米，重568克

2001年邰常来先生捐赠

　　圆形。圆钮，圆钮座。座外八枚圆座小乳钉和"**ℇ**"形纹相间环列。其外围两周凸弦纹。外区等距离分布着七枚圆座乳钉，七乳将镜背分成七区，分别填饰羽人、白虎、玄武、朱雀、独角兽等，细线勾勒，形象生动。其外为铭文圈带："上大山，见神人，食玉英，饮澧泉，驾交龙，乘浮云"。外廓栉齿纹一周。宽缘，缘上饰锯齿纹和云气纹。

Mirror with inscriptions of "Shang Da Shan Jian Xian Ren" and design of seven nipples and mythical animal   Eastern Han Dynasty

Diameter:15.5cm,Thickness of the rim:0.5cm,Weight:568gram

Collected from Mr Tai Changlai in 2001

The mirror is round in shape.It has a round knob on a round base. Outside the base are eight nipples with round base and ℮-shaped patterns arranged alternately.Outside the pattern are two bands of raised string pattern.Outer place of the mirror distribute seven nipples with round base in equidistant which divide the mirror into seven zones with vivid decoration of winged man,White Tiger,Somber Warrior,unicorn and so on.Outside that is a band of inscription "Shang Da Shan,Jian Xian Ren,Shi Yu Ying,Yin Li Quan,Jia Jiao Long,Cheng Fu Yun". Outside the major motif is a band of fine-toothed pattern.On the broad rim is adored with saw pattern and cloud pattern.

神人龙虎画像镜　东汉

直径17.1厘米，边厚0.75厘米，重441克
1985年蚌埠市文物商店移交

　　圆形。圆钮，四叶纹钮座。座外饰双线方框一周。其外在方框四角外置四枚圆座乳钉纹。四乳钉将镜背分四区，两区为一神二侍，神端坐，冠饰不同，二侍双膝跪地，侧身向神。另外两区为一龙一虎，龙虎皆昂首、翘尾、怒目、张口。其外依次饰栉齿纹和锯齿纹各一周。三角缘。

　　纹饰中刻画的两神，应为西王母、东王公的形象，二者为道教神话中的最高神，分别主阴阳。汉代政府虽然推崇儒术，但道教在民间却十分流行，西王母和东王公被视为长生不老的象征。

Mirror with portraits of deity,dragon and tiger Eastern Han Dynasty

Diameter:17.1cm,Thickness of the rim:0.75cm,Weight:441gram

Transferred from antique shops in Bengbu in 1985

The mirror is round in shape.It has a round knob on a base with four leaves design.Outside the base is a square formed by double lines.Outside the four corners of the square are four nipples with base which divide the mirror into four zones.Among which,two zones are adored with a sitting deity wearing different hats and two attendants on their knees and facing to the deity.The other two zones are adored with a dragon and a tiger with heads up,tails rolling up,eyes and mouth opening up.Outside the major motif is a band of fine-toothed pattern and a band of saw pattern.The mirror has a triangular rim.

天王日月铭环状乳神兽镜 东汉

直径12.2厘，边厚1.4厘米，重275克
蚌埠市博物馆旧藏

　　圆形。圆钮，圆钮座。内区主纹为三神三兽相间绕钮环列，其间等距离置八枚环状乳。主神为正面端坐形态，戴冠着袍，两侧环状乳上各一侍者侧身向此神人，另外两神为侧坐态，三兽头部突出，高浮雕的兽首比主神还要明显。外区为半圆、方枚带，半圆枚饰连弧纹，方枚上均铸有"天王日月"四字铭文。边缘纹饰，内为神人禽兽纹带，有六龙驾车、羽人跨青鸟等，外为勾连云纹。

Mirror with inscription of "Tian Wang Ri Yue" and design of annular nipple and mythical animal　Eastern Han Dynasty

Diameter:12.2cm,Thickness of rim:1.4cm,Weight:275gram

Collection of Bengbu Museum

The mirror is round in shape.It has a round knob on a round base.The major motif is three deities and three beasts with protruding heads in high relief arranged inter phase around the knob and eight nipples with round base distribute in same distance.The deity sitting in the middle wearing hat and gown with cape waving.There are two attendants on both sides of the main deity,sitting sideways on a nipple with round base and lean to middle,while the other two deities are sitting sideways.Outside the major motif are two bands of seal,one is semicircle-shaped,the other is square-shaped.On the rim of semicircle-shaped seal is adored with linked arcs design.On the square-shaped seal cast with four inscriptions of "Tian Wang Ri Yue".On the rim of the mirror are two bands of decoration,inner part is a band of deity and beast,including six dragons driving and deity sitting on blue bird.Outer part is a band of linked cloud pattern.

龙虎对峙镜 东汉

直径14.1厘米，边厚0.35厘米，重582克

蚌埠市博物馆旧藏

　　圆形。圆钮，圆钮座。钮的两侧一龙一虎夹钮对峙，龙虎皆采用浅浮雕，身躯部分压在钮座下，龙虎张口、怒目、侧身卷曲。钮下，饰一龟和走兽，龟作回首状，走兽作行走状。其外为铭文圈带，字体漫漶难辨。外围栉齿纹一周。宽缘，缘上饰缠枝花纹一周。

Mirror with design of dragon and tiger facing each other   Eastern Han Dynasty

Diameter:14.1cm,Thickness of Rim:0.35cm,Weight:582gram

Collection of Bengbu Museum

    The mirror is round in shape.It has a round knob on a round base. Around the base is adored with a dragon and tiger facing each other in bas relief,both of which have opening mouth,glaring eyes and rolling body,part of the body is buried by the knob.Below the base is adored with a turtle with head turning back and moving beast.Outside that is a band of inscription with blurry and unclear font.The major motif ends with a band of fine-toothed pattern.The broad rim is adored with a band of interlocking flower pattern.

龙虎对峙镜 东汉

直径11.3厘米，边厚0.9厘米，重374克

蚌埠市博物馆旧藏

　　圆形。圆钮，圆钮座。钮的两侧一龙一虎夹钮对峙，龙虎皆采用高浮雕，身躯部分压在钮下，龙虎张口、吐舌、怒目、侧身卷曲，身躯重点部位饰乳钉加以突出，空白处填以小乳钉装饰。外围两周长短不一的栉齿纹和一周双线波折纹。三角缘。此镜纹饰刻画清晰，龙虎遒劲有力，生动形象。

Mirror with design of dragon and tiger facing each other Eastern Han Dynasty

Diameter:11.3cm,Thickness of Rim:0.9cm,Weight:374gram

Collection of Bengbu Museum

The mirror is round in shape.It has a round knob on a round base. Around the base is adored with a dragon and tiger facing each other in high relief,both of which have opening mouth,glaring eyes and rolling body,part of the body is buried by the knob.The main part of the dragon and tiger's body are decorated with nipple so that the body can be outstanding,while other part of the body are space with small nipples. Outside the major motif are adored with two band of fine-toothed pattern with different lengths and a band of wave pattern formed by double lines.The mirror with a triangular rim,clear casting and exquisite decoration of forceful image,shows a vivid effect.

三虎镜 东汉

直径9.3厘米，边厚0.5厘米，重137克

蚌埠市博物馆旧藏

　　圆形。圆钮，圆钮座。座外浅浮雕式三虎同向绕钮，虎头　　周。三角缘。

硕大，作蹬踏状。其外依次饰栉齿纹、锯齿纹和单线波折纹各一

Mirror with design of three tigers Eastern Han Dynasty

Diameter:9.3cm,Thickness of Rim:0.5cm,Weight:137gram

Collection of Bengbu Museum

The mirror is round in shape.It has a round knob on a round base. Outside the base are three tigers with big head in bas-relief around the knob in one direction,kicking and treading.Outside the major motif is adored with a band of fine-toothed pattern,saw pattern and wave pattern formed by single line in turn.The mirror has a triangular rim.

三虎镜 东汉

直径8.3厘米，边厚0.5厘米，重123克

蚌埠市博物馆旧藏

　　圆形。圆钮，圆钮座。座外浅浮雕式三虎绕钮，其中两虎　　状。其外饰两周长短不一的栉齿纹。三角缘。

对峙，一虎跟随，身躯重点部位饰乳钉加以突出，三虎皆作蹬踏

Mirror with design of three tigers Eastern Han Dynasty

Diameter:8.3cm,Thickness of Rim:0.5cm,Weight:123gram

Collection of Bengbu Museum

The mirror is round in shape.It has a round knob on a round base. Outside the base are three tigers kicking and treading in bas relief around the knob,among which,two tigers are facing each other,the last one is following.The body part of the tigers are decorated with nipples to outstanding.Outside the major motif is adored with two bands of fine-toothed pattern with different lengths.The mirror has a triangular rim.

三虎镜 东汉

直径9.4厘米，边厚0.65厘米，重192克

蚌埠市博物馆旧藏

　　圆形。圆钮，圆钮座。座外浅浮雕式三虎绕钮，其中两虎　　状。其外饰两周长短不一的栉齿纹和一周单线波折纹。三角缘。

对峙，一虎跟随，身躯重点部位饰乳钉加以突出，三虎皆作蹬踏

Mirror with design of three tigers   Eastern Han Dynasty

Diameter:9.4cm,Thickness of Rim:0.65cm,Weight:192gram

Collection of Bengbu Museum

The mirror is round in shape.It has a round knob on a round base. Outside the base are three tigers kicking and treading in bas relief around the knob,among which,two tigers are facing each other,the last one is following.The body part of the tigers are decorated with nipples to outstanding.Outside the major motif is adored with two bands of fine-toothed pattern with different lengths and a band of wave pattern formed by single line.The mirror has a triangular rim.

三虎镜 东汉

直径9.9厘米，边厚0.8厘米，重214克

蚌埠市博物馆旧藏

　　圆形。圆钮，圆钮座。座外浅浮雕式三虎绕钮，其中两虎　　状。其外饰两周长短不一的栉齿纹和一周单线波折纹。三角缘。
对峙，一虎跟随，身躯重点部位饰乳钉加以突出，三虎皆作蹭踏

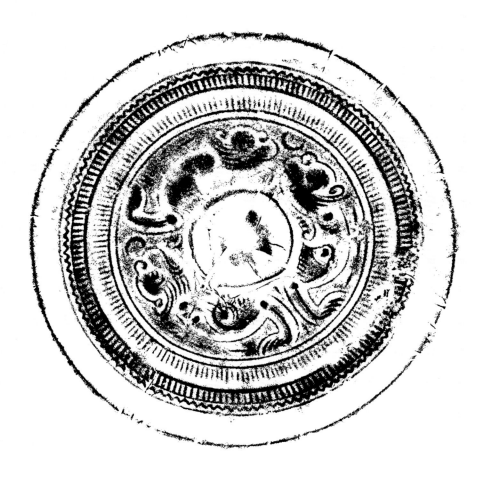

Mirror with design of three tigers   Eastern Han Dynasty

Diameter:9.9cm,Thickness of Rim:0.8cm,Weight:214gram

Collection of Bengbu Museum

The mirror is round in shape.It has a round knob on a round base. Outside the base are three tigers kicking and treading in bas relief around the knob,among which,two tigers are facing each other,the last one is following.The body part of the tigers are decorated with nipples to outstanding.Outside the major motif is adored with two bands of fine-toothed pattern with different lengths and a band of wave pattern formed by single line.The mirror has a triangular rim.

三虎镜 东汉

直径11厘米，边厚1.5厘米，重364克

1994年怀远县施长田先生送交

圆形。圆钮，圆钮座。座外高浮雕式三虎绕钮，其中两虎对峙，一虎跟随，身躯重点部位饰乳钉加以突出，三虎皆作蹬踏状。外饰铭文圈带"龙氏作竟四夷（服），多贺君家人民息，胡羌殄（灭）天下复，风（雨）时节"。外饰一周栉齿纹。宽缘，缘上饰锯齿纹和双线波折纹。

此镜铸造精致，纹饰清晰，高浮雕的装饰手法让龙虎的形象更加生动。镜铭存在减字省字现象，其内容反映出两汉时期，北方匈奴不断南下，导致战乱不断，人民生活苦不堪言的历史背景以及内心渴望安定和平的美好愿望。

Mirror with design of three tigers Eastern Han Dynasty

Diameter:11cm,Thickness of Rim:1.5cm,Weight:364gram

Transferred by Mr. Shi Changtian from Huanyuan country in1994

The mirror is round in shape.It has a round knob on a round base. Outside the base are three tigers kicking and treading in bas relief around the knob,among which,two tigers are facing each other,the last one is following. The body part of the tigers are decorated with nipples to outstand.Outside that is adored with a band of inscription "Long Shi Zuo Jing Si Yi (Fu),Duo He Jun Jia Ren Min Xi,Hu Qiang Zhen (Mie) Tian Xia Fu,Feng (Yu) Shi Jie".The major motif ends with a band of fine-toothed pattern.The broad rim is decorated with saw pattern and wave pattern formed by double lines.

The mirror with clear design and exquisite decoration in high relief shows a vivid image of dragon and tiger.The inscriptions on the mirror are not complete,some words are omitted.Its contents reflect the historic background of lasting war between the two Han Dynasties and Xiongnu Nation,people were suffering an unspeakable life and they desired for peace and stability in the deep heart.

位至三公铭龙凤纹镜　六朝
直径11厘米，边厚0.27厘米，重160克
1975年征集

　　圆形。圆钮，圆钮座。钮座上下两条竖线间各饰"位至"和"三公"铭文，钮左侧饰一只"S"形曲体凤鸟，右侧饰一条"S"形曲体龙。外围一周栉齿纹。素宽缘。

　　三公，是对天子之下的最高管理者的称呼，辅佐天子，是中国古代朝廷中最尊显的三个官职的合称。两汉时期，人们把"位至三公"作为追求高官厚禄，以达荣华富贵的最高目标。铜镜上铸刻"位至三公"，反映了当时人们的价值取向和社会观念。

Mirror with inscription of "Wei Zhi San Gong" and design of dragon and phoenix　The Six Dynasties
Diameter:11cm,Thickness of Rim:0.27cm,Weight:160gram
Collected in 1975

　　The mirror is round in shape.It has a round knob on a round base. Above and below the knob are two vertical lines with inscriptions of "Wei Zhi" and "San Gong" inside,on the left side of the knob is adored with a S-shaped phoenix while right side of the knob is decorated with a S-shaped dragon.Outside the major motif is a band of fine-toothed pattern.The mirror has a broad rim without design.

　　San Gong,the highest management under the charge of Emperor whose function is assist the king,is an union calling for the most three honorable positions in ancient Chinese court.During the two Han Dynasties,people treat San Gong as their pursuit of high position and handsome salary to the final goal of splendid wealth and glory. Inscription of "Wei Zhi San Gong" on the mirror reflect people's values and social thoughts at that time.

对置式神兽镜　六朝

直径11.6厘米，边厚0.35厘米，重211克

1985年蚌埠市东区砖室墓出土

　　圆形。圆钮，连珠纹钮座。主纹分四组：两组为一神二兽，对置；另两组各一神人。其外置十二个方形枚和十二个半圆形枚相间环列，枚上铭文，模糊难辨，之间点缀珠纹。边缘有铭文圈带，字体模糊，难以辨识。此镜整体纹饰和铭文呈现一种模糊感，系镜范多次使用所致。

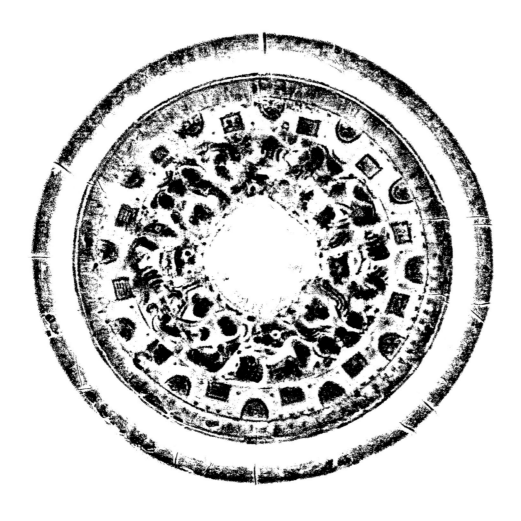

Mirror with opposite design of deities and beasts   The Six Dynasties

Diameter:11.6cm,Thickness of Rim:0.35cm,Weight:211gram

Unearthed from a brick tomb in east region of Bengbu City in 1985

The mirror is round in shape.It has a round knob on a base with design of linked beads.The major motif comprise four groups:the two groups with same patterns of a deity and two beasts are opposite,the other two groups cast with a deity only.Outside that alternate arrangement of twelve square-shaped seals and twelve half round shaped seals with vague inscriptions on and adored with bead pattern in the space.On the rim is a band of inscription with vague font.Because of the repeated use of mirror mold,the patterns and inscriptions on the mirror show a vague sense and hard to recognize.

赏得秦王铭四瑞兽镜　唐代

直径9.1厘米，边厚0.8厘米，重221克
蚌埠市博物馆旧藏

　　圆形。圆钮。一周高凸弦纹将镜背分为内外两区。内区四只瑞兽绕钮奔跑，四兽均昂头翘尾，四肢舒展。外区为铭文圈带："赏得秦王镜，判不惜千金，非关欲照胆，特是自明心。"点线纹缘。

　　铭文上关于"秦王"的典故，有两个说法，一说指秦始皇，在阿旁宫的入口处悬挂一面巨大的铜镜，传说铜镜可以照胆，对人有震慑作用，秦始皇用它来照出怀有异心的觐见者或刺客；一说指即位前封为秦王的唐太宗李世民，《贞观政要·论任贤》："夫以铜为镜，可以正衣冠；以古为镜，可以知兴替；以人为镜，可以明得失。朕常保此三镜，以防己过。今魏征殂逝，遂亡一镜矣。"

Mirror with inscription of "Shang De Qin Wang" and design of four auspicious animals　Tang Dynasty

Diameter:9.1cm,Thickness of Rim:0.8cm,Weight:221gram
Collection of Bengbu Museum

　　The mirror has a round shape and a round knob.Its back side is divided into two parts by a band of high raised string pattern.Inner part is adored with four running auspicious beasts with heads and tails up,four legs stretch.Inner part is inscription band "Shang De Qin Wang Jing,Pan Bu Xi Qian Jin,Fei Guan Yu Zhao Dan,Te Shi Zi Ming Xin". The rim is decorated with line pattern formed by points.

　　There are two arguments about the allusion of Emperor Qin,one refers to the first Emperor of Qin,he put a huge mirror at the entrance of E Pang Palace to pick out disloyal audience or assassin;one refers to the Emperor Taizong of the Tang,Li Shimin,who was dubbed King of Qin before he ascended the throne.As recorded in Zhenguan Politicians on Appointing Sage,with bronze as a mirror,one can rectify dress;with history as a mirror,one can know dynasties changed;with person as a mirror,one can understand advantages and disadvantages.I often keep the three mirrors on hands to prevent the mistakes.Now Wei Zheng die away,I lost a good mirror".

四瑞兽葡萄镜 唐代

直径9.4厘米，边厚1厘米，重305克
蚌埠市博物馆旧藏

　　圆形。伏兽钮。一周高凸弦纹将镜背分为内外两区。内区高浮雕四瑞兽，伏卧于葡萄枝蔓中，瑞兽首尾相连，形态各异；外区为葡萄枝蔓和果实、禽鸟相间环列，葡萄果实粒粒饱满，禽鸟形态各异，有的振翅飞翔，有的伫立休憩。叠云纹缘。

　　葡萄镜的纹样源于西域，《金石索》载："海马蒲桃竟，博古图不释其意，或取天马徕自西极及张骞使得蒲桃归之异欤？"唐代时，葡萄广泛种植，葡萄纹样也开始流行。瑞兽纹饰在中国自有传统，六朝、隋、初唐铜镜上瑞兽盛行。瑞兽葡萄镜把瑞兽和葡萄合在一起，再加上鸟禽花枝相应，呈现出一幅生动活泼的画面：祥云瑞兽，翻腾闹海，葡萄串枝，藤蔓鹊绕，优美轻快。

Mirror with design of four auspicious animals and grapes Tang Dynasty

Diameter:9.4cm,Thickness of Rim:1cm,Weight:305gram

Collection of Bengbu Museum

　　The mirror is round in shape.It has a squatting beast-shaped knob with realistic head.ts back side is divided into two parts by a band of high raised string pattern.Inner part is adored with four auspicious beasts in high relief with head and tail connected,ambushing among the branches full of plump grapes in various shapes.Outer part decorate with branches full of grapes and birds which casted in various shapes of flying or standing.The mirror has a rim with overlap clouds pattern.

　　From the record of Jin Shisuo we know that the pattern of grapes came from western regions and grapes were brought by Zhang Qian to China in the reign of Emperor Wu of the Han Dynasty.When Tang Dynasty,grapes were widely planted and grape pattern began to popular.The auspicious beasts pattern has a long historical tradition and it prevailed from Six Dynasties to Sui and early Tang.Mirror with design of auspicious beast and grape is the combine of the two patterns,coupled with birds,flowers and branches,which showing up a vivid and animate picture:propitious cloud and auspicious beasts are running and playing in the sea,magpie flying around the branches full of grapes with graceful and beautiful pose.

五瑞兽葡萄镜　唐代

直径12厘米，边厚1.3厘米，重574克

蚌埠市博物馆旧藏

　　圆形。伏兽钮。一周高凸弦纹将镜背分为内外两区。内区高浮雕五瑞兽，伏卧于葡萄枝蔓中，瑞兽首尾相连，形态各异；外区为葡萄枝蔓和果实、禽鸟相间环列，葡萄果实粒粒饱满，禽鸟形态各异，有的振翅飞翔，有的伫立休憩。叠云纹缘。

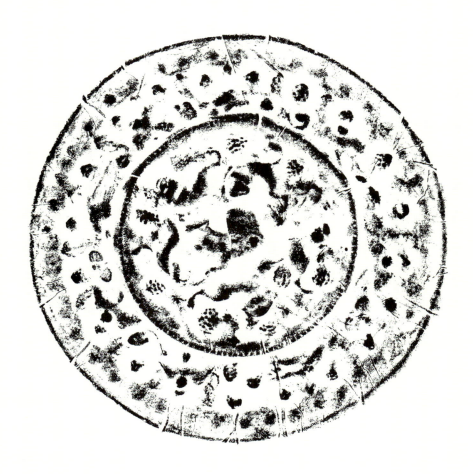

Mirror with design of five auspicious animals and grapes Tang Dynasty
Diameter:12cm,Thickness of Rim:1.3cm,Weight:574gram
Collection of Bengbu Museum

The mirror is round in shape.It has a squatting beast-shaped knob with realistic head.Its back side is divided into two parts by a band of high raised string pattern.Inner part is adored with five auspicious beasts in high relief with head and tail connected,ambushing among the branches full of grapes in various shapes.Outer part decorate with branches full of plump grapes and birds which casted in various shapes of flying or standing.The mirror has a rim with overlap clouds pattern.

瑞兽鸾鸟绕花枝镜 唐代

直径11厘米，边厚0.6厘米，重325克

蚌埠市博物馆旧藏

八瓣菱花形。圆钮，钮外饰四蜂蝶。再外为两瑞兽、两禽鸟与四花枝相间环列。钮的左右各饰一只鸾鸟，鸾鸟振翅飞翔，尾翼伸展。钮的上下各饰一只瑞兽，两瑞兽作同向奔跑状，上瑞兽头上有双角，身有羽翼。两兽尾部皆翘起。禽鸟和瑞兽均做同向绕钮运动。边缘八瓣处饰八朵折枝花。窄缘。

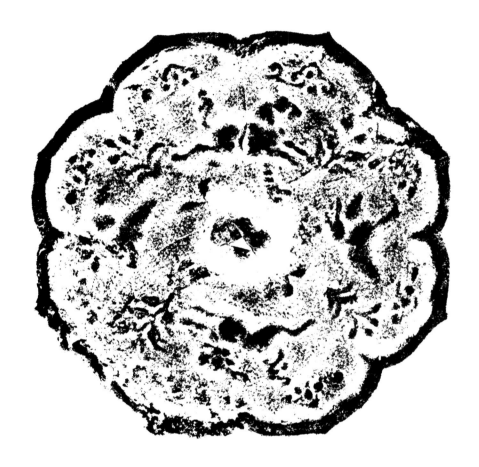

Mirror with design of auspicious animals,phoenixes and interlocking flowers Tang Dynasty

Diameter:11cm,Thickness of Rim:0.6cm,Weight:325gram

Collection of Bengbu Museum

The mirror is in shape of eight-petal water chestnut and has a round knob.Outside the knob is adored with four bees and butterflies. Then alternate arrangement of two auspicious beasts,two birds and four branches with flowers.Both right and left sides of the knob decorate with a flying phoenix with tail widely opening up.Both top and bottom of the knob decorate with a auspicious beast running in same direction. The beast on the top side has two horns and wings.Both two auspicious beast's tail are perking up.Decoration of bird and beast are in same direction around the knob.On the edge of eight-petal are eight branches of flower.The mirror has a narrow rim.

雀绕花枝镜　唐代

直径9.5厘米，边厚0.4厘米，重162克

蚌埠市博物馆旧藏

　　八瓣菱花形。圆钮。高齿纹圈将镜背分为内外两区，内区四雀飞绕小花枝，外区四雀飞绕大花枝，八雀均同向。素窄缘。

Mirror with design of magpie flying around the flowers   Tang Dynasty

Diameter:9.5cm,Thickness of Rim:0.4cm,Weight:162gram

Collection of Bengbu Museum

The mirror is in shape of eight-petal water chestnut and has a round knob.Its back side is divided into two parts by a band of raised tooth-shaped pattern.Inner part is adored with four magpies flying around the small flowering branches,while outer part is adored with four magpies flying around big flowering branches.All eight magpies are flying in the same direction.The mirror has a narrow rim without design.

雀绕花枝镜　唐代

直径10厘米，边厚0.5厘米，重175克
1974年本市征集

　　八瓣菱花形。圆钮。钮外四禽鸟四折枝花相间环绕。四禽鸟各两组，一组两鹊振翅飞翔，尾翼伸展；一组两雁双脚站立，羽翼未张。四禽鸟间有形状稍异的两组折枝花对称分布。主题纹饰营造出一副安静祥和的画面，是唐代盛世之下，人们热爱生活、享受太平的真实写照。边缘展翅的四蜂蝶与四朵两叶一苞的折枝花相间排列。窄缘。

Mirror with design of magpie flying around the flowers　Tang Dynasty

Diameter:10cm,Thickness of Rim:0.5cm,Weight:175gram
Collection from Bengbu City in 1974

　　The mirror is in shape of eight-petal water chestnut and has a round knob.Outside the knob alternate arrangement of four birds and four flowering branches.Four birds are divided into two groups,among which,one group of two magpies flying high with wings opening up and tails stretching while the other group of two wild geese standing on two feet with wings closed.There are two groups of flowering branches in various shapes spaced in the four birds in a symmetrical distribution.The major motif creates a quiet and peaceful picture which is a true portrayal of people who love life and enjoy the peace under the background of flourishing Tang Dynasty.Inside each petal of the rim is decorated with alternate arrangement of bees,butterflied and flowering branches with two buds and one leaf.The mirror has a narrow rim.

雀绕花枝镜　唐代

直径4.9厘米，边厚0.7厘米，重305克

蚌埠市博物馆旧藏

　　八瓣菱花形。圆钮。钮外四禽鸟四折枝花相间环绕。四禽鸟各两组，一组两鹊振翅飞翔，尾翼伸展；一组两雁振翅飞翔，头颈伸长。四禽鸟间有四朵相同的两叶两苞的折枝花相间分布。边缘展翅的四蜂蝶与四朵两叶两苞的折枝花相间排列。窄缘。唐代铜镜纹饰趋于写实，贴近生活，此镜描绘了一幅安逸祥和的画面，反映了盛唐时期人们的价值取向和社会观念。

Mirror with design of magpie flying around the flowers　Tang Dynasty

Diameter:4.9cm,Thickness of Rim:0.7cm,Weight:305gram

Collection of Bengbu Museum

　　The mirror is in shape of eight-petal water chestnut and has a round knob.Outside the knob alternate arrangement of four birds and four flowering branches.Four birds are divided into two groups,one group of two magpies flying high with wings opening up and tails stretching ,while the other group of two wild geese flying high with heads and necks stretching ahead.Between the four birds are four flowering branches with two leaves and two buds arranged alternately. On the edge of major motif are four flying bees and butterflies and four flowering branches with two leaves and two buds which arranged alternately.Patterns on Tang Mirror tend to realism and close to life,this mirror describe a comfortable and peaceful picture which reflect people's value and social thought in Tang Dynasty.

双鸾双瑞兽镜 *唐代*

直径16.7厘米，边厚0.45厘米，重550克

蚌埠市博物馆旧藏

　　圆形。圆钮，花瓣钮座。钮的左右各饰一只鸾鸟，曲颈相　　兽，上为天马，下为麒麟，两瑞兽作同向奔跑状，天马头上有双
对，振翅而立，尾羽后翘，尾部覆羽卷起。钮的上下各饰一只瑞　　角，身有羽翼，两兽尾部皆翘起。素窄缘。

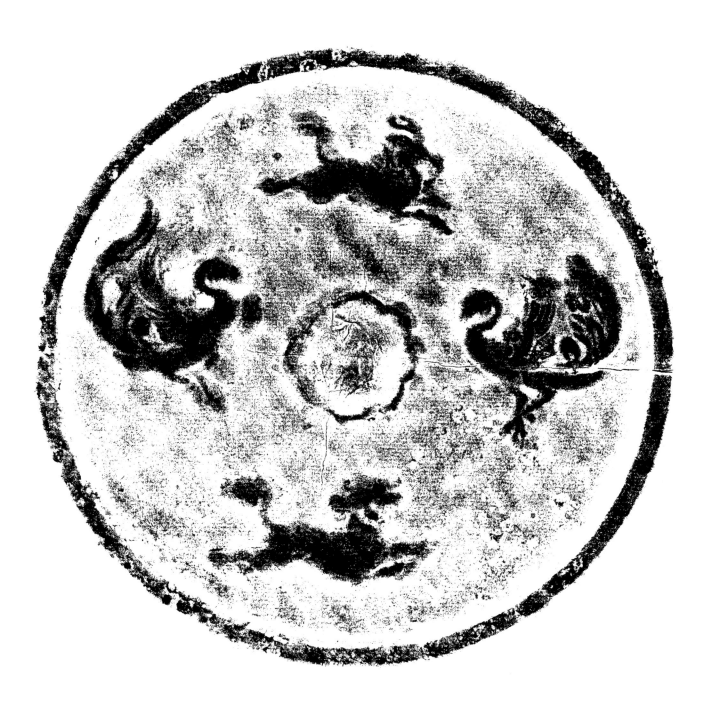

Mirror with design of double phoenixes and double auspicious animals   Tang Dynasty

Diameter:16.7cm,Thickness of Rim:0.45cm,Weight:550gram

Collection of Bengbu Museum

The mirror is round in shape.It has a round knob a petal-shaped base.Both right and left sides of the knob is adored with a standing phoenix facing each other with wings opening,feathers on the tail rolling up and tails perking up.On the top and bottom part of the knob is decorated with a auspicious beast running in the same direction,among that,top part is a horse with two horns and wings,while bottom part is a Chinese unicorn with tail perking up.The mirror has a narrow rim without design.

双鸾双瑞兽镜 唐代
直径16.3厘米，边厚0.5厘米，重900克
蚌埠市博物馆旧藏

　　八出葵花形。圆钮，花瓣钮座。钮的左右各饰一只鸾鸟，曲颈相对，振翅而立，尾羽后翘，尾部覆羽卷起。钮的上下各饰一只瑞兽，上为天马，下为麒麟，两瑞兽作同向奔跑状，天马头上有双角，身有羽翼，两兽尾部皆翘起。素窄缘。

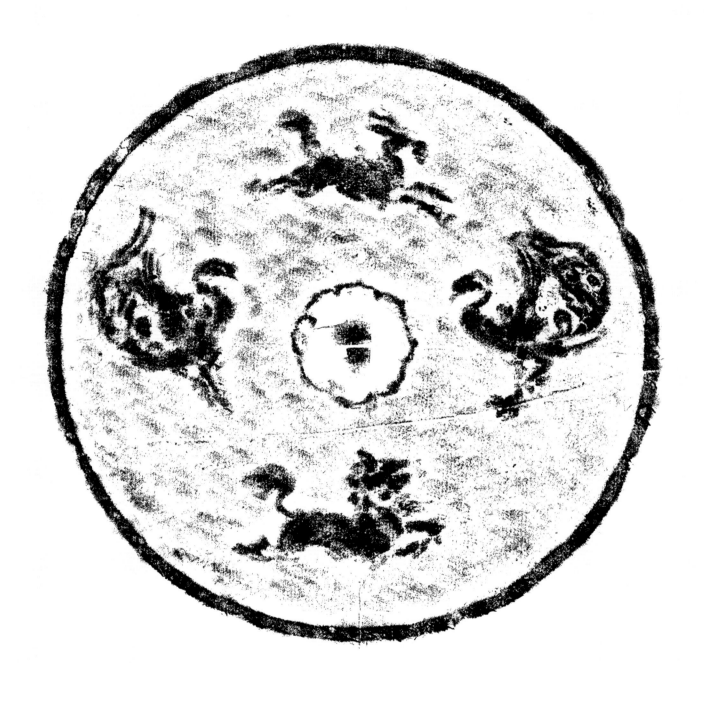

Mirror with design of double phoenixes and double auspicious animals Tang Dynasty

Diameter:16.3cm,Thickness of Rim:0.5cm,Weight:900gram

Collection of Bengbu Museum

The mirror is in shape of eight-petal mallow.It has a round knob on a petal-shaped base.Both right and left sides of the knob is adored with a standing phoenix facing each other with wings opening,feathers on the tail rolling up and tails perking up.On the top and bottom part of the knob is decorated with a auspicious beast running in the same direction,among that,top part is a horse with two horns and wings,while bottom part is a Chinese unicorn with tail perking up.The mirror has a narrow rim without design.

双鸾双鸟衔绶镜　唐代
直径17.4厘米，边厚0.45厘米，重610克
蚌埠市博物馆旧藏

　　八出葵花形。圆钮。钮的两侧各饰一只衔绶鸾鸟，鸾鸟曲颈相对，振翅而立，足踏莲花宝枝，绶尾向上飘起；钮的上下各饰一只飞鸟，同向飞行，上鸟双翼向上振起，口衔葡萄枝实，下鸟双翼平展，口衔一长绶带。外饰一周凸弦纹。边缘处四组带苞花叶和四蜂蝶相间环绕。窄缘。

　　双鸾衔绶，是唐代的流行的一种吉祥纹饰，通常为双鸾相对飞翔，口衔挽结长绶，配以鲜花祥云。"鸾"是民间传统中象征吉祥的飞鸟，"长绶"象征"长寿"（同音），绶带挽结，表示永结同心。

Mirror with design of double phoenixes and double birds holding ribbons Tang Dynasty

Diameter:17.4cm,Thickness of Rim:0.45cm,Weight:610gram

Collection of Bengbu Museum

The mirror is in shape of eight-petal mallow and has a round knob.Both right and left sides of the knob is adored with a phoenix holding ribbons,facing each other,stepping on lotuses,spreading wings and dancing,tails perking up.The knob is decorated with a bird opening up its wings and holding grapes on the top and a bird opening flatly its wings and holding a long ribbon,both which are flying toward the same direction.Inside each petal of the rim is decorated with alternate arrangement of flowers,bees and butterflies.The mirror has a narrow rim.

Patterns of double phoenixes holding ribbons is an auspicious decoration popular in Tang dynasty.The pattern was usually designed into phoenixes flying facing each other,holding a knotting ribbons in its mouth,decorate with flowers and auspicious clouds.Phoenix is the symbol of auspicious and lucky bird in ancient China,long ribbon stands for long life(same pronunciation),ribbon with knot means couples are tying together and have the same heart.

双鸾衔绶花鸟镜 唐代

直径13.2厘米，边厚0.5厘米，重364克

蚌埠市博物馆旧藏

　　八出葵花形。圆钮。钮的左右各饰一只鸾鸟，双鸾同形，口衔长绶，足踏花枝，振翅翘尾，夹钮相对。钮上饰一株两叶一苞花，钮下饰一只踏枝云雀，作回首状。边缘八瓣折枝花与云纹相间环列。窄缘。此镜制作精美，纹饰刻画细致入微，禽鸟形象极富动感。

Flower-bird-shaped mirror with design of double phoenixes holding ribbons Tang Dynasty

Diameter:13.2cm,Thickness of Rim:0.5cm,Weight:364gram

Collection of Bengbu Museum

The mirror is in shape of eight-petal mallow and it has a round knob.Both right and left sides of the knob is adored with a phoenix holding ribbons,facing each other around the knob,stepping on flowering branches,spreading wings,perking tails.The knob is decorated with a flower which has two buds and a leaf on the top and a magpie stepping on a branch which looking back.Inside each petal of the rim is decorated with alternate arrangement of flowering branches and clouds pattern.The mirror has a narrow rim with delicate cast and exquisite decoration,which shows a energetic bird's image.

双鸾衔绶镜 唐代

直径13.3厘米，边厚0.3厘米，重301克
1999年凤阳县大庙镇出土

　　圆形。圆钮。钮的两侧各饰一只鸾鸟，首尾相对，鸾鸟双翅　　成花结，两端有连珠。窄缘。
扇起，拖着细长的尾羽，羽翅挺劲。各衔一长绶带，绶带中间打

Mirror with double birds holding ribbons Tang Dynasty

Diameter:13.3cm,Thickness of Rim:0.3cm,Weight:301gram

Unearthed at Damiao Village Fengyang country in1999

   The mirror is round in shape and has a round knob.Both sides of the knob are decorated with two phoenixes which has a long and powerful tail.One's head connects with another head,spreading wings and dancing,holding a long ribbon with knot in the middle and linked beads at the ends.The mirror has a narrow rim.

四花四鹊镜 唐代

直径18.6厘米，边厚0.6厘米，重925克

蚌埠市博物馆旧藏

六出葵花形，弧度极小，圆钮。钮外环绕四蜂蝶，再外为四丛花枝及四喜鹊相间环列。四花各两组，一组长宽条叶，一组

叶片较小，叶上均衬托出盛开的花瓣。四鹊均作飞翔状，双翅张开，尾翼伸展。素窄缘。

Mirror with design of four flowers and four magpies Tang Dynasty

Diameter:18.6cm,Thickness of Rim:0.6cm,Weight:925gram

Collection of Bengbu Museum

The mirror is in shape of six-petal mallow with minimal curvature and has a round knob.Outside the knob circled with four butterflies,then outside the butterflies are decorated with alternate arrangement of four flowering branches and four magpies.Four flowers are divided into two groups,one group of flowers has long and wide leaves while the other group has small leaves,on all leaves are blooming flowers.All four magpies are flying with wings widely open,tails stretch.The mirror has a narrow rim without design.

四花四鹊镜 唐代
直径18.9厘米，边厚0.5厘米，重950克
蚌埠市博物馆旧藏

　　六出葵花形，弧度极小。圆钮。钮外环绕四蜂蝶，再外为四丛花枝及四喜鹊相间环列。四花各两组，一组长宽条叶，一组叶片较小，叶上均衬托出盛开的花瓣。四鹊均作飞翔状，双翅张开，尾翼伸展。素窄缘。

　　花枝镜流行于盛唐时期，纹饰典雅端庄，反映了唐代国力强盛、文化繁荣，社会欣欣向荣的景象。

Mirror with design of four flowers and four magpies Tang Dynasty

Diameter:18.9cm,Thickness of Rim:0.5cm,Weight:950gram

Collection of Bengbu Museum

The mirror is in shape of six-petal mallow with minimal curvature and has a round knob.Outside the knob circled with four butterflies,then outside the butterflies are decorated with alternate arrangement of four flowering branches and four magpies.Four flowers are divided into two groups,one group of flowers has long and wide leaves while the other group has small leaves,on all leaves are blooming flowers.All four magpies are flying with wings widely open,tails stretch.The mirror has a narrow rim without design.

Mirror with flowers was popular in Tang Dynasty,the elegant decoration shows a flouring society with strong national power and cultural prosperity.

折枝花鸟镜 唐代

直径21.8厘米，边厚0.5厘米，重1252克

蚌埠市博物馆旧藏

　　圆形。圆钮，花瓣钮座。座外四花枝绕钮排列，花枝为五叶一苞的折枝花，形态一致，绽蕊怒放，每一花枝下饰一鹊，形态或展翅，或作回首状。四花枝之间饰一两叶一苞的小折枝花。素缘。

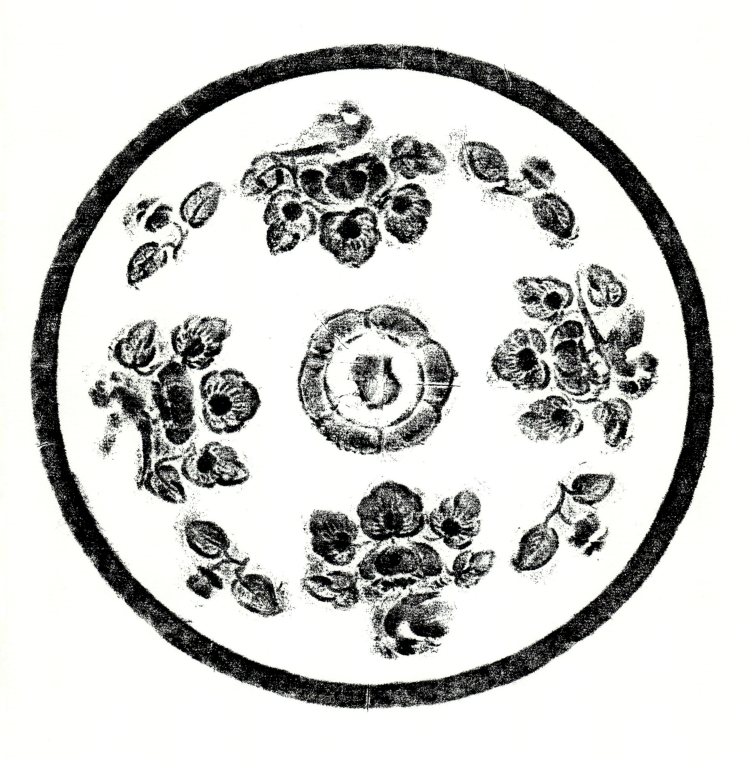

Mirror with design of interlocking flowers and birds Tang Dynasty

Diameter:21.8cm,Thickness of Rim:0.5cm,Weight:1252gram

Collected from Bengbu City in 1975

The mirror is round in shape.It has a round knob on a petal-shaped base.The major motif is the design of four flowers which are adored with five leaves and one bud design,in the space are decorated with small branch with leaves and bud.Below each flower has a magpie in various shapes,flying or stepping and turning around.The mirror has a rim without design.

折枝花鸟镜　唐代

直径21.6厘米，边厚0.55厘米，重1445克
蚌埠市博物馆旧藏

　　八出葵花形。圆钮，花瓣钮座。座外四花枝绕钮排列，花枝为五叶一苞的折枝花，形态一致，绽蕊怒放，每一花枝下饰一鹊，形态或展翅，或作回首状。四花枝之间饰一两叶一苞的小折枝花。素缘。

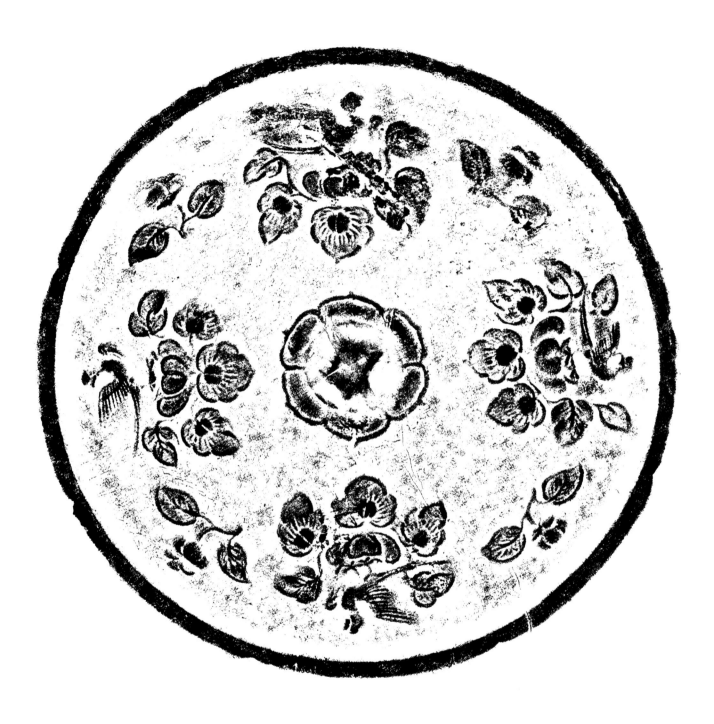

Mirror with design of interlocking flowers and birds Tang Dynasty

Diameter:21.6cm,Thickness of Rim:0.55cm,Weight:1445gram

Collection of Bengbu Museum

The mirror is in shape of eight-petal mallow.It has a round knob on a petal-shaped base.The major motif is the design of four flowers which are adored with five leaves and one bud design,in the space are decorated with small branch with leaves and bud.Below each flower has a magpie in various shapes,flying or stepping and turning around. The mirror has a rim without design.

六花枝镜 唐代

直径21.5厘米，边厚0.75厘米，重1150克
蚌埠市博物馆旧藏

　　圆形。圆钮，花瓣钮座。座外围一周凸弦纹。其外六株大花　　一种叶中鲜花展瓣错综掩映。素缘。
枝环绕，花枝为两种各三组。一种枝头绽蕾吐芬，花头向荣。另

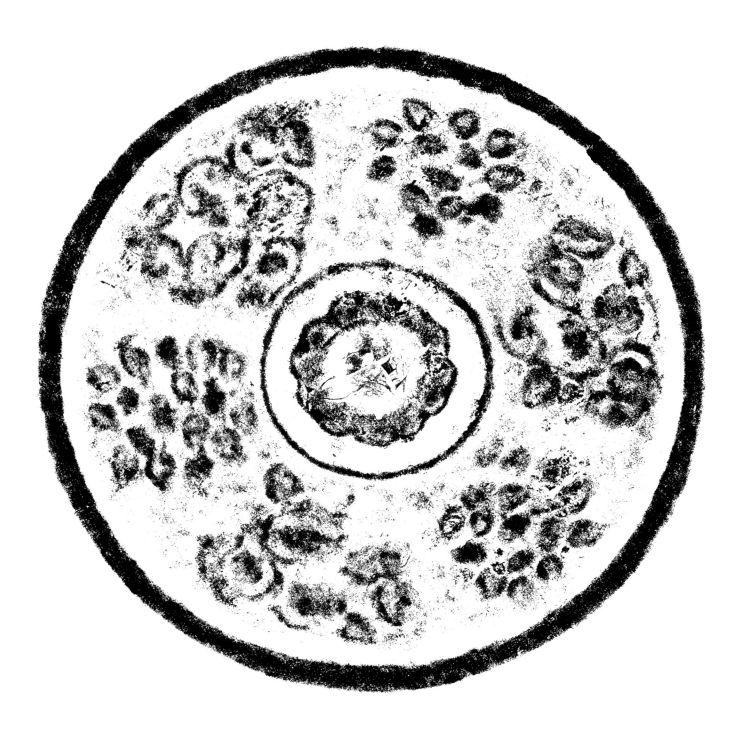

Mirror with design of six flowers Tang Dynasty
Diameter:21.5cm,Thickness of Rim:0.75cm,Weight:1150gram
Collection of Bengbu Museum

The mirror is in round shape.It has a round knob on a petal-shaped base.Outside the base is a band of raised string pattern.The major motif are six flowers with two shapes in three groups around the base.One kind is flowers blooming on the top of branch,the other kind is flowers and leaves arranged alternately.The mirror has a rim without design.

宝相花镜 唐代

直径14厘米，边厚0.35厘米，重284克

蚌埠市博物馆旧藏

　　圆形。桥钮，花瓣钮座。座外等距离分布六朵花卉纹，花卉纹分两组，一组六瓣，一组十二瓣，相间分布，花中置花蕊。素窄缘。

　　宝相花，隋唐时期佛教装饰中盛行的一种花卉图案。一般以象征富贵的牡丹，象征纯洁的荷花，象征坚贞的菊花为主体，中间镶嵌着形状不同、大小粗细有别的其他花叶组成。尤其在花芯和花瓣基部，用圆珠作规则排列，像闪闪发光的宝珠，故名"宝相花"。

Mirror with rosette design Tang Dynasty

Diameter:14cm,Thickness of Rim:0.35cm,Weight:284gram

Collection of Bengbu Museum

The mirror is round in shape.It has a bridge-shaped knob on a petal-shaped base.Its back side is adored with six flower patterns with six petals arranging in the same distance outside the base.The patterns are divided into two groups which are alternately arranged,one group of flower with six petals while the other group with twelve petals.Each flower carved with black spots in the middle which stand for stamen. The mirror has a narrow rim without design.

Rosette is a popular flower in Buddhism decoration during Sui and Tang Dynasties.The pattern is usually take peony which is the symbol of wealth,lotus which stand for pure,chrysanthemum which symbolize faith and loyalty as the theme of decoration with leaves in various shapes and different sizes.In the flower core and bottom of petals decorated with beads in regular arrangement just like shining pearls,so we called the flower as rosette(means like treasure).

宝相花镜　*唐代*

直径13.9厘米，边厚0.25厘米，重300克
蚌埠市博物馆旧藏

　　圆形。圆钮，花瓣钮座。座外等距离分布六朵花卉纹，花卉纹
分两组，一组六瓣，一组十二瓣，相间分布，花中置花蕊。素窄缘。

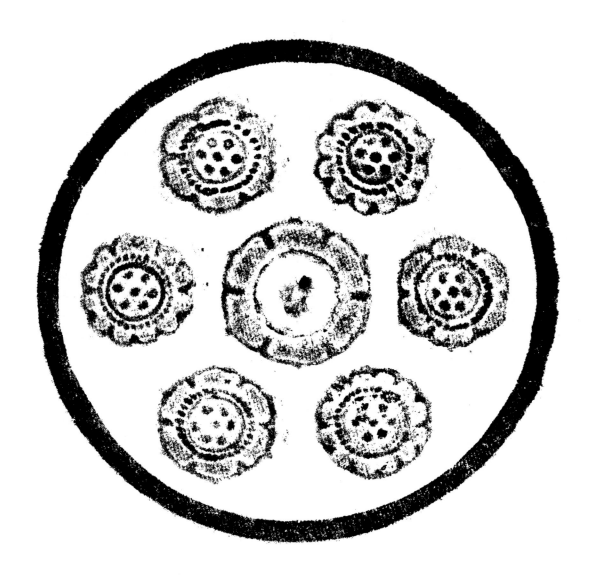

Mirror with rosette design Tang Dynasty

Diameter:13.9cm,Thickness of Rim:0.25cm,Weight:300gram

Collection of Bengbu Museum

    The mirror is round in shape.It has a bridge-shaped knob on a petal-shaped base.Its back side is adored with six flower patterns with six petals arranging in the same distance outside the base.The patterns are divided into two groups which are alternately arranged,one group of flower with six petals while the other group with twelve petals.Each flower carved with black spots in the middle which stand for stamen. The mirror has a narrow rim without design.

宝相花镜 唐代

直径13.8厘米，边厚0.35厘米，重251克

蚌埠市博物馆旧藏

　　圆形。桥钮，花瓣钮座。座外等距离分布六朵莲花，六朵莲花分为两组，相间排布。一组为六瓣莲花，另一组为十二瓣莲花。花中圆圈内七个点代表花蕊，圆圈外饰连珠纹一周。素窄缘。

Mirror with rosette design Tang Dynasty

Diameter:13.8cm,Thickness of Rim:0.35cm,Weight:251gram

Collection of Bengbu Museum

　　The mirror is round in shape.It has a bridge-shaped knob on a petal-shaped base.Its back side is adored with six flower patterns with six petals arranging in the same distance outside the base.The patterns are divided into two groups which are alternately arranged,one group of flower with six petals while the other group with twelve petals.Each flower carved with black spots in the middle which stand for stamen. The mirror has a narrow rim without design.

宝相花镜 唐代

直径11.8厘米，边厚0.4厘米，重139克

蚌埠市博物馆旧藏

　　八出葵花形。圆钮，花瓣钮座。座外等距离分布八朵花卉　　中置花蕊；另一组为旋转式六瓣花，花中置花蕊。素窄缘。
纹。花卉纹分两组，每组四朵，相间环列。一组为六瓣莲花，花

Mirror with rosette design Tang Dynasty

Diameter:11.8cm,Thickness of Rim:0.4cm,Weight:139gram

Collection of Bengbu Museum

　　The mirror is in shape of eight-petal mallow. It has a round knob on a petal-shaped base.Its back side is adored with eight flowers arranging in the same distance.The flowers are divided into two groups,each group has four flowers arranged alternately.Among them,one is in shape of a lotus with six petals and stamen in the middle;the other is in shape of a blooming flower consisting of the center with six petals and stamen in the middle.The mirror has a narrow rim without design.

真子飞霜镜　唐代

直径21厘米，边厚0.55厘米，重1200克

蚌埠市博物馆旧藏

　　八出葵花形。龟钮，荷叶形钮座。钮左一人峨冠博带，坐而抚琴，前设香案，后依竹林。钮右一凤鸟，振翅翘尾舞于石上，其上有树两株。钮上为云上日月出，钮下为石山水池，水波涟漪，池内伸曲柄荷叶，叶上突出一龟，正好形成镜钮。素缘。

　　关于真子飞霜镜所反映的含义，目前尚无定论，一说认为"真子"即"真孝子"的简称，"飞霜"为古琴曲调十二操之一，《履霜操》的别称，讲述的是在周宣王时期尹伯奇被放逐于野的传说。

Mirror with design of Zhen Zi play the zither Tang Dynasty

Diameter:21cm,Thickness of Rim:0.55cm,Weight:1200gram

Collection of Bengbu Museum

The mirror is in shape of eight-petal mallow. It has a tortoise-shaped knob on a base with design of lotus leaf.On the left side of the knob is adored with a man wearing a top hat and wide clothes with belts,sitting before a censer table and bamboos forest behind,playing the zither.On the right side of the knob is adored with a phoenix spreading wings and tail, dancing on a stone,above the phoenix are two trees.The knob is decorated with sun and moon in the cloud on the top and stone,mountain,pool with ripples at the bottom.In the pool is adored with a stretching bent lotus leaf with a tortoise on it,which formed the knob.

There is no exact determine about the meaning which the mirror reflect.Some scholar believe that Zhen Zi is the short one for Zhen Xiao Zi,while Fei Shuang is also mamed Lv Ji Cao,one of the famous twelve melodies of ancient zither which telling the story about Yin Boqi was exiled in the wild by the King Xuan of the Zhou.

交枝四花镜 五代

直径11.2厘米，边厚0.3厘米，重95克
蚌埠市博物馆旧藏

　　圆形。圆钮，菊花纹钮座。座外围凸弦纹两周。其外四株交　　花头相对，细枝长叶。花枝外围三周凸弦纹。素宽缘。
枝花环列一周，花枝交叠，枝头一朵盛开花瓣。四株交枝花两两

Mirror with design of four interlocking flowers The Five Dynasty
Diameter:11.2cm,Thickness of Rim:0.3cm,Weight:95gram
Collection of Bengbu Museum

The mirror is round in shape.It has a round knob on a chrysanthemum-shaped base.Outside the base is adored with two bands of raised string pattern.Outside the string band is adored with a band of four interlocking flowers around the base.Flowers are blooming,overlapping and facing each other on the fine branches with long leaves.Outside the flowers are three bands of raised string.The mirror has a broad rim without rim.

刘思训造铭省坊镜 五代

直径16.1厘米，边厚0.25厘米，重342克

1986年淮光乡仇家岗张功胜先生送交

　　圆形。圆钮。钮外环一周双连珠纹构成的大方框，框内饰连钱纹。两组连珠纹间的空白处，左右两侧各铸有四字铭文"省坊镜面，刘思训造"；上下部各填饰四组花卉纹；方框四角填饰四组钱纹。框外满铺龟背纹。两周连珠纹为廓。素宽缘。

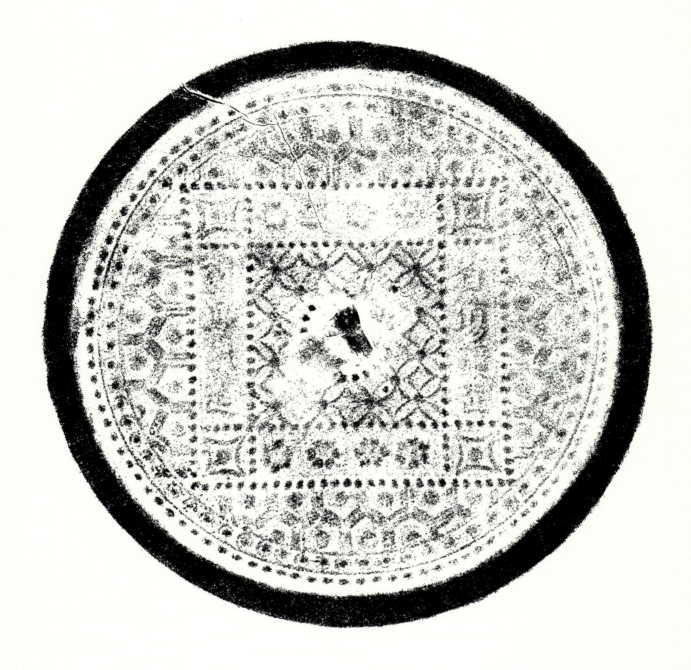

Sheng-fang mirror with inscription of "Liu Si Xun Zao"   The Five Dynasty

Diameter:16.1cm,Thickness of Rim:0.25cm,Weight:342gram

Transferred by Mr Zhang Gongsheng from Qiujia Hillock,Huaiguang Village in 1986

The mirror is round in shape and has a round knob.Outside the knob is a square formed by double linked beads pattern with linked coins decoration inside the square.There are four inscriptions "Sheng Fang Jing Mian" in the right blank between the double linked beads pattern,while the four "Liu Si Xun Zao" in the left side of the blank.

Above and below the base are spaced with four groups of flower pattern;four corners of the square are adored with four coin patterns. Outside the square is full of turtle-backed pattern.Outside the major motif are two bands of linked beads pattern.The mirror has a broad rim without design.

素镜　　五代

直径14.5厘米，边厚0.3厘米，重285克

1976年凤阳县小溪河公社第八队郁汉杰先生送交

　　亚字形。圆钮。通体素面，无纹饰。素宽缘。此镜素雅庄重，不施粉黛，却别具一番韵味。

Mirror without design　　The Five Dynasty

Diameter:14.5cm,Thickness of Rim:0.3cm,Weight:285gram

Transferred by Mr Yu Hanjie from the Eighth Team,small River Commune,Fengyang Country in 1976

　　The mirror is in shape of Ya character and has a round knob. The mirror is adored without design and has a broad rim.The mirror is solemn and elegant without makeup but full of charm.

双凤镜 五代

直径9.9厘米，边厚0.3厘米，重123克

1980年长丰县代集公社杨湖大队许东和先生送交

　　圆形。桥钮。钮的两侧各饰一只凤鸟，首尾相对，双凤均振翅绕钮飞翔，尾翼伸展。外围一周连珠纹。素宽缘。

Mirror with double phoenixes design　The Five Dynasty

Diameter:9.9cm,Thickness of Rim:0.3cm,Weight:123gram

Transferred by Mr Xu Donghe from Yanghu Team,Daiji Commune in Changfeng country in1980

　　The mirror is round in shape and has a bridge-shaped knob. Each side of the knob is adored with a phoenix flying around the knob with wings and tail spreading.One phoenix's head connect to another phoenix's tail.Outside the major motif is a band of linked beads pattern. The mirror has a broad rim without design.

双凤镜 宋代

直径26厘米，边厚1.4厘米，重1800克

蚌埠市博物馆旧藏

　　圆形，圆钮。双凤绕钮对飞，形态一致。双凤头顶有矮冠羽，细颈弯曲，双翅伸展，身上羽毛丰满，尾翼细长飘逸。双凤之间填充云气纹。外围一周凸弦纹，窄缘。此镜双凤羽翅刻画细致，形态逼真，整个图案线条纤细、精致美观，整个画面给人一种轻松浪漫的感觉，体现出宋代匠师的卓越技艺。

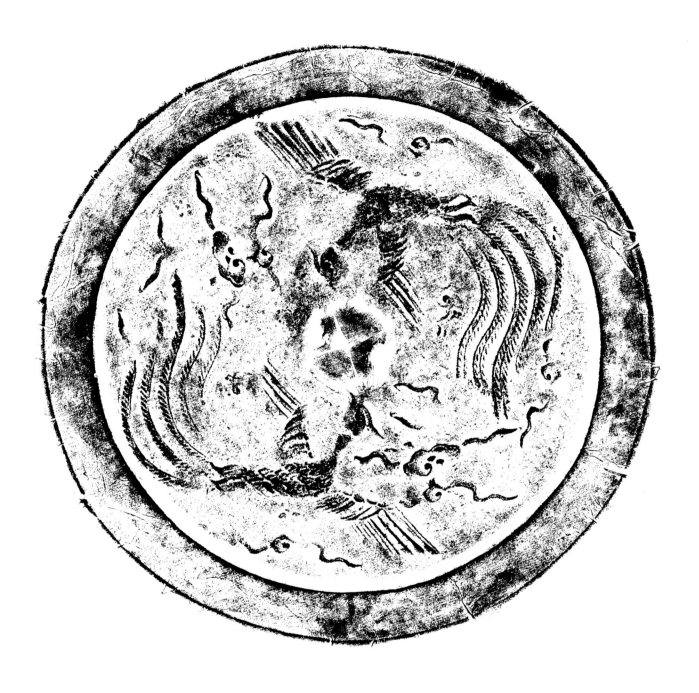

SMirror with double phoenixes design Song Dynasty

Diameter:26cm,Thickness of Rim:1.4cm,Weight:1800gram

Collection of Bengbu Museum

The mirror is round in shape and has a round knob.It is decorated with two vivid phoenixes with short crest flying around knob,thin neck bending,wings spreading.Between the two phoenixes are spaced cloud design.Outside the major motif is adored with a raised string pattern and a narrow rim.The phoenix with delicate feathers and vivid shape shows an easy and romantic felling which reflect excellent craftmanship in Song Dynasty.

双凤带柄镜　宋代

直径12.8厘米，执柄长10.4厘米，宽1.5厘米，重561克
蚌埠市文物商店移交

　　八出葵花形。长柄。镜背双凤对飞，双凤皆细颈弯曲，羽翼　　却将双凤的形象展示的栩栩如生。窄缘。
丰满，尾羽伸展，满铺镜背。整个画面不留白，线条繁密复杂，

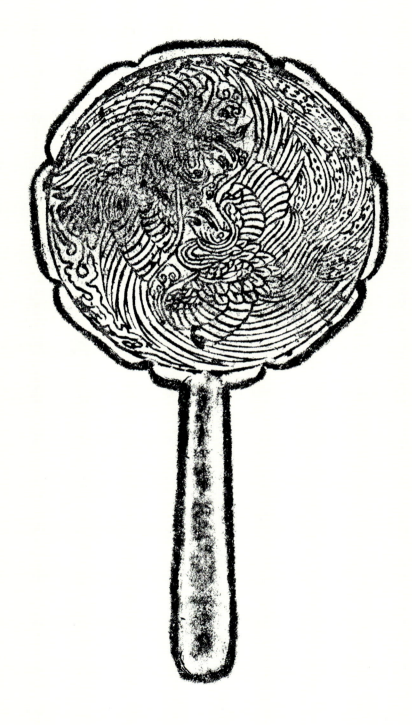

Mirror with handle and double phoenixes design Song Dynasty

Diameter:12.8cm,Length of handle:10.4cm,Width:1.5cm,Weight:561gram

Collection of Bengbu Museum

The mirror is in shape of eight-petal mallow and has a long handle.The mirror is adored with two full-fledged phoenixes flying back to back,both necks bending and tails spreading,full of the mirror back.The whole mirror full of dense and complex lines without any blank but shows a vivid phoenix image.The mirror has a narrow rim.

双鱼镜　宋代
直径11.6厘米，边厚0.5厘米，重110克
1976年本市征集

　　圆形。平顶小圆钮。钮的左右各饰一翘首张口、展鳍摆尾、　　直线水草纹。外置一周凸弦纹。窄缘。
作腾跃状的鲤鱼纹，两鱼形态一致，头尾相接。钮的上下饰两条

Mirror with design of double fish Song Dynasty

Diameter:11.6cm,Thickness if rim:0.5cm,Weight:110gram

Collected from Bengbu City in 1976

The mirror has a round shape and a thin body.It has a round knob with flat top.There are two fish,which are raising heads,opening mouths,spreading fins and swinging tails,at both sides of the knob. Above and below the knob are decorated with two straight water weed design.A band of raised string pattern surrounds the major motif.The mirror has a narrow rim.

缠枝四花镜　宋代
直径14.8厘米，边厚0.1厘米，重200克
1975年本市征集

　　亚字形。桥形小钮，花瓣钮座。座外环绕四朵缠枝花，花头对着亚字形的内角。边缘内侧饰一周连珠纹。素宽平缘。此镜构图枝叶连亘、互相缠绕，画面细致，描绘逼真，具有强烈的现实感和韵律节奏感。

Mirror with design of four interlocking flowers   Song Dynasty

Diameter:14.8cm,Thickness of rim:0.1cm,Weight:200gram

Collected from Bengbu City in1975

The mirror is in shape of Ya character.It has a bridge-shaped knob on a petal-shaped base.Outside the base are adored with four interlocking flowers head towards the four corners of Ya character.Inner side of the rim is decorated with a band of linked beads pattern.The rim without design is broad and has a flat surface.The mirror with delicate decoration of interlocking flowers and leaves has a strong sense of realty and rhythm.

菊花纹四花镜　宋代

边长7.6厘米，边厚0.3厘米，重100克

蚌埠市博物馆旧藏

　　方形。钮残，菊花纹钮座。座外两周凸弦纹间饰一周连珠纹。

四株折枝花置于方形四内角处，花瓣均向钮开放。素宽平缘。

Mirror with design of chrysanthemum and four flowers   Song Dynasty

Length:7.6cm,Thickness of rim:0.3cm,Weight:100gram

Collection of Bengbu Museum

The mirror is rectangle in shape.It has a incomplete knob on a base with design of chrysanthemum.Outside the base is adored with two bands of raised string pattern with a band of linked bead pattern in the space.The four corners of the rectangle are decorated with four interlocking flowers which blooming towards the knob.The rim without design is broad and has a flat surface.

草叶纹四花镜　宋代

边长12.8厘米，边厚0.2厘米，重234克

蚌埠市博物馆旧藏

　　方形。桥形小钮。钮外环列两组八边形凸弦纹。其外围一周浮雕式草叶纹圈带，草叶纹圈带外方镜的内四角处各饰一株折枝花，折枝花外环"∟"形草叶纹带，其间空白处饰四株小折枝花。边缘内侧环绕一周连珠纹。素宽平缘。

Mirror with design of grass-leaf and four flowers   Song Dynasty

Length:12.8cm,Thickness of rim:0.2cm,Weight:234gram

Collection of Bengbu Museum

The mirror is rectangle in shape and has a bridge-shaped knob. Outside the knob are two bands of octagon-shaped raised string pattern. Outside the octagon is a band of grass-leaf pattern in relief,between the grass-leaf pattern and the four inner corners of the mirror are adored with four interlocking flowers.Outside the interlocking flower is adored with a band of ∟-shaped grass-leaf design which spaced with four small interlocking flowers.The major motif is surrounded with a band of linked beads pattern.The rim without design is broad and has a flat surface.

许由巢父故事镜　宋代

直径18厘米，边厚0.8厘米，重1250克

蚌埠市博物馆旧藏

　　圆形。圆钮，钮顶平。镜背上部是几座巍峨峭拔峰峦，中　　牛，一人坐地，两人作对话姿态。素宽平缘。
峰顶端一树枝虬干曲，垂于山腰。镜背下部，山脚下河边一人牵

Mirror with pattern of legendary incident of Xu You and Chao Fu Song Dynasty

Diameter:18cm,Thickness of rim:0.8cm,Weight:1250gram

Collection of Bengbu Museum

The mirror is round in shape.It has a round knob with a flat top. The half part above the knob is adored with several lofty mountains,on the top of middle mountain planting a tree with branches hanging till the hillside.The below part is casting with two talking people,one is sitting,the other one is holding a cattle.The rim without design is broad and has a flat surface.

湖州真石家铭葵花镜　宋代

直径10.3厘米，边厚0.3厘米，重84.5克

蚌埠市博物馆旧藏

　　六出葵花形。钮残。钮左侧置一长方形框，框内铸两行铭

文："湖州真石家／念二叔照子。"窄缘。

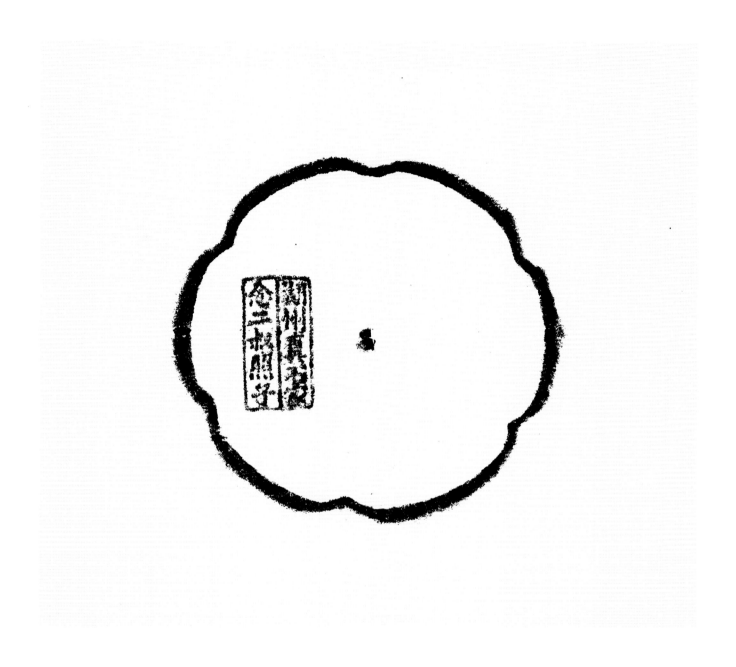

Mallow-shaped mirror with inscription of "Hu Zhou Zhen Shi Jia" Song Dynasty

Diameter:10.3cm,Thickness of rim:0.3cm,Weight:84.5gram

Collection of Bengbu Museum

The mirror is in shape of six-petal mallow and has a incomplete knob.At the left side of the knob is a rectangle with inscription "Hu Zhou Zhen Shi Jia Nian Er Shu Zhao Zi" in two vertical lines.The mirror has a narrow rim.

湖州真石家铭葵花镜　宋代

直径14.9厘米，边厚0.3厘米，重302克

蚌埠市博物馆旧藏

　　六出葵花形。桥形小钮。钮右侧置一长方形框，框内
铸两行铭文："湖州真石家／念二叔照子。"窄缘。

Mallow-shaped mirror with inscription of "Hu Zhou Zhen Shi Jia" Song Dynasty

Diameter:14.9cm,Thickness of rim:0.3cm,Weight:302gram

Collection of Bengbu Museum

The mirror is in shape of six-petal mallow and has a bridge-shaped knob.At the right side of the knob is a rectangle with inscription "Hu Zhou Zhen Shi Jia Nian Er Shu Zhao Zi"in two vertical lines.The mirror has a narrow rim.

湖州李家铭葵花镜　宋代

直径11.8厘米，边厚0.5厘米，重139克

蚌埠市博物馆旧藏

六出葵花形。桥形小钮。钮左侧置一长方形框，框内铸两行
铭文："湖州李家真／炼铜照子记"。窄缘。

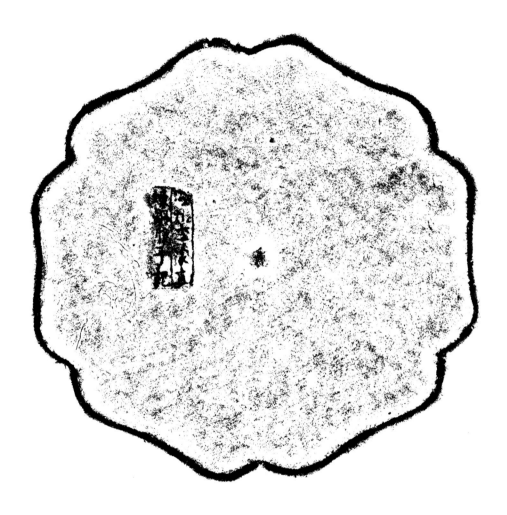

Mallow-shaped mirror with inscription of "Hu Zhou Li Jia" Song Dynasty

Diameter:11.8cm,Thickness of rim:0.5cm,Weight:139gram

Collection of Bengbu Museum

The mirror is in shape of six-petal mallow and has a bridge-shaped knob.At the left side of the knob is a rectangle with inscription "Hu Zhou Li Jia Zhen Lian Tong Zhao Zi Ji" in two vertical lines.The mirror has a narrow rim.

湖州仪枫桥石家铭葵花镜　宋代

直径11.8厘米，边厚0.3厘米，重139克

蚌埠市博物馆旧藏

　　八出葵花形。小圆钮。钮左侧置一长方形框，框内铸两行铭
文："湖州仪枫桥石家／真正一色青铜镜。"素宽缘。

Mallow-shaped mirror with inscription of "Hu Zhou Yi Feng Qiao Shi Jia"　Song Dynasty

Diameter:11.8cm,Thickness of rim:0.3cm,Weight:139gram

Collection of Bengbu Museum

　　The mirror is in shape of eight-petal mallow and has a round knob.At the left side of the knob is a rectangle with inscription "Hu Zhou Yi Feng Qiao Shi Jia Zhen Zheng Yi Se Qing Tong Jing" in two vertical lines.The mirror has a broad rim without design.

湖州仪枫桥石家铭葵花镜　宋代
直径12.8厘米，边厚0.3厘米，重168克
蚌埠市博物馆旧藏

　　八出葵花形。小圆钮。钮右侧置一长方形框，框内铸两行铭
文："湖州仪凤桥石家／真正一色青铜镜。"素宽缘。

Mallow-shaped mirror with inscription of "Hu Zhou Yi Feng Qiao Shi Jia" Song Dynasty

Diameter:12.8cm,Thickness of rim:0.3cm,Weight:168gram

Collection of Bengbu Museum

The mirror is in shape of eight-petal mallow and has a small round knob.At the right side of the knob is a rectangle with inscription "Hu Zhou Yi Feng Qiao Shi Jia Zhen Zheng Yi Se Qing Tong Jing" in two vertical lines.The mirror has a broad rim without design.

湖州石念二叔铭镜　宋代

直径11.8厘米，边厚0.5厘米，重139克

蚌埠市博物馆旧藏

　　亚字形。小圆钮。钮右侧置一长方形框，框内铸两行铭文：
"湖州石念二／叔青铜照子。"素缘。

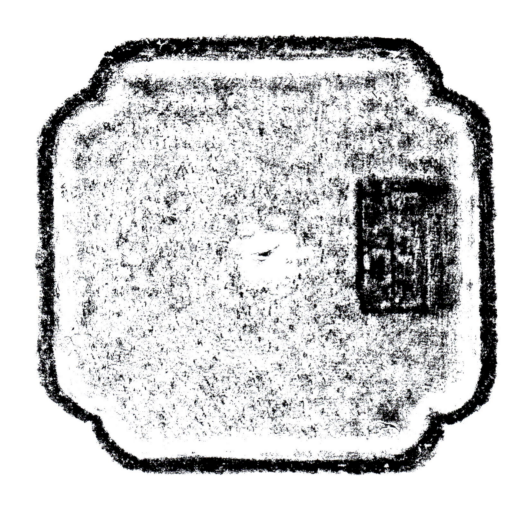

Mirror with inscription of "Hu Zhou Shi Nian Er Shu" Song Dynasty

Diameter:11.8cm,Thickness of rim:0.5cm,Weight:139gram

Collection of Bengbu Museum

The mirror is in shape of Ya character and has a small round knob.At the the right side of the knob is a rectangle with inscription "Hu Zhou Shi Nian Er Shu Qing Tong Zhao Zi" in two vertical lines.The mirror has a rim without design.

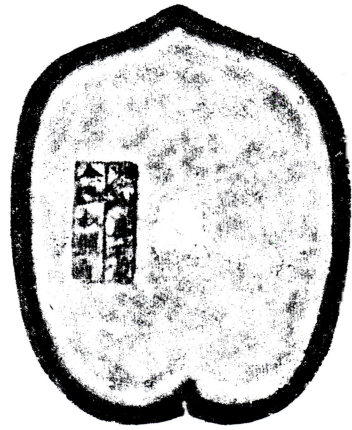

湖州真石家铭桃形镜　宋代

宽9.8厘米，高12.7厘米，边厚0.3厘米，重290克
蚌埠市博物馆旧藏

　　桃形。桥形小钮。钮左侧置一长方形框，框内铸两行铭文：
"湖州真石家／念二叔照子。"窄缘。

Peach-shaped Mirror with inscription of "Hu Zhou Zhen Shi Jia"　Song Dynasty

Width:9.8cm,Height:12.7cm,Thickness of rim:0.3cm,Weight:290gram
Collection of Bengbu Museum

　　The mirror is in shape of a peach and has a bridge-shaped knob. At the left side the knob is a rectangle with inscription "Hu Zhou Zhen Shi Jia,Nian Er Shu Zhao Zi" in two vertical lines.The mirror has a narrow rim.

湖州真正方家铭桃形镜 宋代

宽8.9，高10.9厘米，边厚0.4厘米，重130克

蚌埠市博物馆旧藏

　　桃形。桥钮。钮左侧置一长方形框，框内铸两行铭文："湖州真正方家／炼铜无比照子。"窄缘。

Peach-shaped Mirror with inscription of "Hu Zhou Zhen Zheng Fang Jia" Song Dynasty

Width:8.9cm,Height:10.9cm,Thickness of rim:0.4cmWeight:130gram

Collection of Bengbu Museum

　　The mirror is in shape of a peach and has a bridge-shaped knob. At the left side the knob is a rectangle with inscription "Hu Zhou Zhen Zheng Shi Jia,Lian Tong Wu Bi Zhao Zi" in two vertical lines.The mirror has a narrow rim.

双鱼镜 金代

直径11.8厘米，边厚0.2厘米，重139克

蚌埠市博物馆旧藏

　　圆形。桥钮。钮上下各饰一鲤鱼，鱼体肥大，摇头摆尾，首　　内铸铭文"镜子局官□"。窄缘。

尾相接，空白处填饰水波纹。钮左靠镜缘处置一长方形方框，框

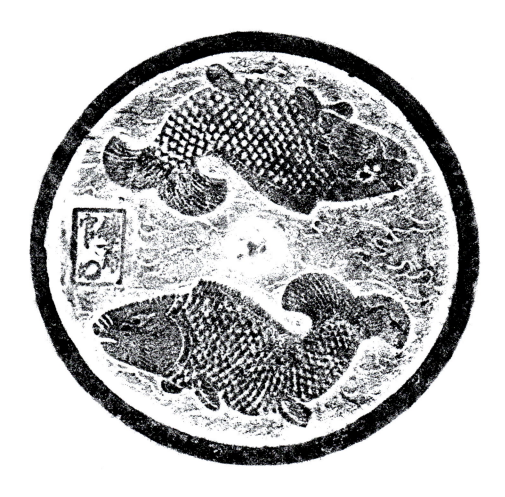

Mirror with design of double fish   Jin Dynasty

Diameter:11.8cm,Thickness of rim:0.2cm,Weight:139gram

Collection of Bengbu Museum

The mirror is round in shape and has a bridge-shaped knob. There are two fat carps,which are raising heads,opening mouths,spreading fins and tails,at both sides of the knob.The carps are spaced with ripple pattern.At the left side of the knob that close the rim is a rectangle with inscription "Jing Zi Ju□".The mirror has a narrow rim.

双鱼带柄镜 金代

直径11厘米，边厚0.45厘米，重288克

蚌埠市博物馆旧藏

　　圆形，柄残。龟钮。钮的两侧各饰一鲤鱼，两鱼头尾相接，　　弦纹和缘之间饰一周流动回旋水草纹带。宽缘。

侧身摆尾，绕钮游动，空白处填以水波纹作装饰。外饰凸弦纹，

Mirror with handle and double fish design   Jin Dynasty

Diameter:11cm,Incomplete length of handle:0.4cm,Width of handle:2cm, Thickness of rim:0.45cm,Weight:288gram

Collection of Bengbu Museum

The mirror is round in shape and has an incomplete knob. There are two carps,which are raising heads,opening mouths,spreading fins and tails,at both sides of the knob.The carps are spaced with water wave pattern.Outside the major motif is a band of raised string pattern. Between the string pattern and the broad rim is adored with a band of flowing and swirling water weed pattern.

摩羯纹带柄镜　金代

径10.5厘米，执柄长9.7厘米，柄宽1.9厘米，边厚0.7厘米，重575克

蚌埠市博物馆旧藏

　　桃形，长柄。镜背高浮雕饰一摩羯展翅高飞，翱翔于翻滚的海面。上方祥云中露出一弯新月。素窄凸缘。摩羯(makara)，梵语译音，为佛教语，源于印度。摩羯传入中国后，经过中国佛教的重新诠释，形象演变为龙首鱼身，成为佛教中的一种神鱼，是如来佛在水中的化身。

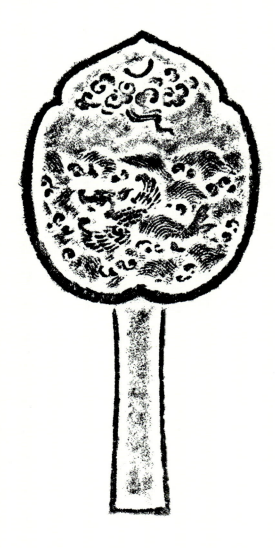

Mirror with handle and makara pattern   Jin Dynasty

Diameter:10.5cm,Length of handle:6.5cm,Width of handle:1.9cm,Thickness of rim:0.7cm,Weight:575gram

Collection of Bengbu Museum

The mirror is in shape of a peach and has a long handle.The mirror back is adored with a makara flying on the surging sea.On the above part of the mirror back is adored with a crescent in the auspicious clouds.The mirror has a narrow rim without design.The word makara is translated by its Sanskrit pronunciation.After makara being transmitted to China,it has been reinterpreted by Chinese Buddhist,and got the image of Dragon-like head and fish-like body.Makara becomes a fish god and is the Buddha's transformation in water form.

缠枝四花镜　金代

径10.8厘米，边厚0.2厘米，重100克

蚌埠市博物馆旧藏

　　亚字形。小圆钮，钮顶平。座外环绕四朵缠枝花。边缘内侧
饰一周连珠纹。素宽平缘。缘上有錾刻，为简笔字，难以辨认。

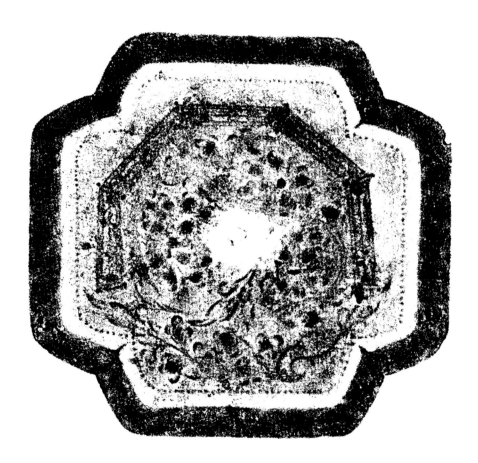

Mirror with design of four interlocking flowers   Jin Dynasty

Diameter:10.8cm,Thickness of rim:0.2cm,Weight:100gram

Collection of Bengbu Museum

The mirror is in shape of a Ya character and has a small knob with flat top.Outside the base are are adored with four interlocking flowers around.Inner part of the rim is decorated with a band of linked beads pattern.The rim without design is broad and has a flat surface. On the rim is engraved characters with simplified strokes and hard to recognize.

莲花纹带柄镜　金代

直径13.5厘米，执柄长9.7厘米，柄宽2.1厘米，边厚0.35厘米，重213克

蚌埠市博物馆旧藏

　　圆形，长柄。镜背用单线条勾勒出三朵绽放的莲花，居中的莲　　一朵小莲花。素窄凸缘。

花稍大，下部装饰一荷叶，荷叶硕大，叶下为水波，两侧分别伸出

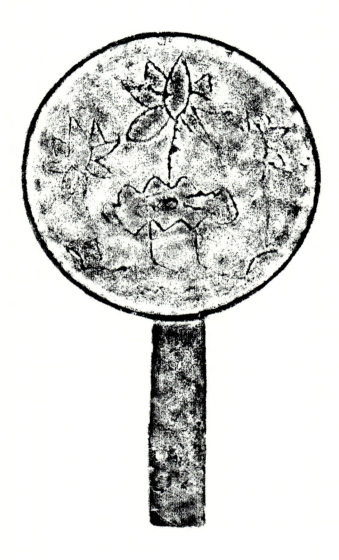

Mirror with handle and lotus design Jin Dynasty

Diameter:13.5cm,Length of handle:9.7cm,Width of handle:2.1cm,Thickness of rim:0.35,Weight:213gram

Collection of Bengbu Museum

The mirror is round in shape with a long handle.The major motif is three blooming lotuses drawing with single line,the one in the middle has a bigger size with two huge lotus leaves at the bottom,under the leaves is flowing water.The narrow rim showing no design and rolling.

高山流水人物镜 金代
直径16厘米，边厚0.4厘米，重467克
蚌埠市博物馆旧藏

　　圆形。圆钮，钮顶平。钮上中心处置一单线方框，框外为山峦、树木。钮右侧一瀑布从山石间一泻而下，直入钮下方的水潭之中。钮左一人倚石临溪坐于山坳之中，抬头远望飞流直下的瀑布，神态悠闲。外环一周凸棱。素宽平缘。

Mirror with patterns of high mountains,flowing water and figure   Jin Dynasty

Diameter:16cm,Thickness of rim:0.4cm,Weight:467gram

Collection of Bengbu Museum

The mirror is round in shape and has a round knob with flat top. At the middle part above the knob is placing a square formed by single line,outside the square are mountains and trees.A waterfall between rocks is on the right side of the knob,which is flowing down into the poll at the bottom.A man by the river is sitting and leaning on the rocks,enjoying the scene of waterfall with comfortable looking.The major motif is surrounded with a band of raised string pattern.The rim without design is broad and has a flat surface..

镜子局官□铭镜　金代

直径11.4厘米，边厚0.2厘米，重114克

蚌埠市博物馆旧藏

　　六出葵花形。桥钮，钮顶平。钮右侧置一长方形方框，框内铸

铭文"镜子局官□"。窄缘。

Mirror with inscription of "Jing Zi Ju Guan□" Jin Dynasty

Diameter:11.4cm,Thickness of rim:0.2cm,Weight:114gram

Collection of Bengbu Museum

The mirror is in shape of six-petal mallow and has a bridge-shaped knob with a flat top.At the right side of the knob is a rectangle with inscription "Jing Zi Ju Guan□".The mirror has a narrow rim.

吴牛喘月故事镜　金代

直径19.2厘米，边厚0.45厘米，重800克

蚌埠市博物馆旧藏

　　圆形。圆钮。钮上中间出置一单线方框。其外天空中烟云映带，一弯新月。水天相接，翻滚的层层波浪，占据镜背的大部分。钮的左右两侧各有一仙人，手托宝盘。钮下水中一牛，翘首张望，呼呼喘气。素宽平缘。

　　吴牛，指江淮一带的水牛。吴地天气多炎暑，生于江南的水牛，怕热，见到月亮以为是太阳，望月而喘。

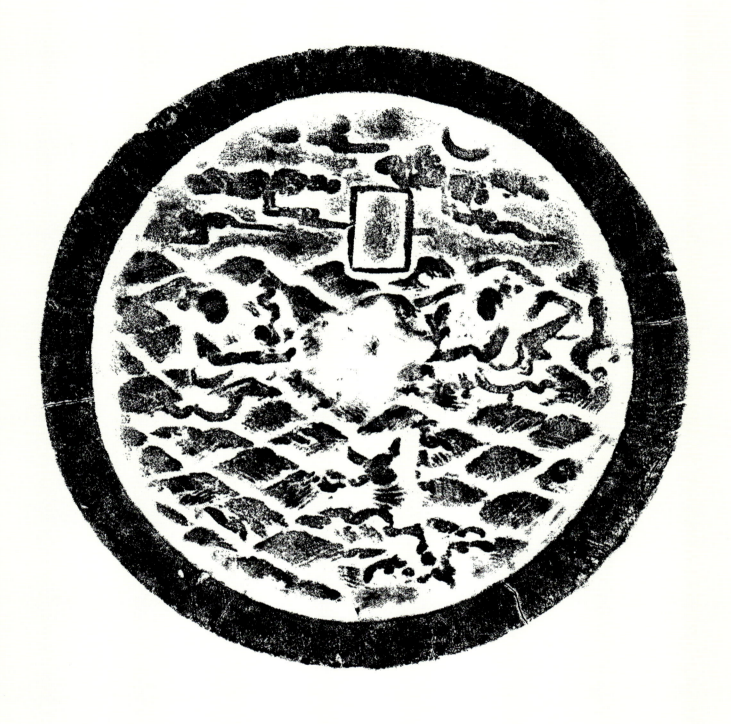

Mirror with pattern of legendary incident of Wu buffalo panting to the moon Jin Dynasty

Diameter:19.2cm,Thickness of rim:0.45cm,Weight:800gram

Collection of Bengbu Museum

The mirror is round in shape and has a round knob.At the middle part above the knob is placing a square formed by single line,outside the square are clouds and crescent in the sky.Rolling water and clouds are connecting which occupy the most part of the mirror.Each side of the knob is adored with a deity holding a treasure dish.Below the knob is a buffalo in the water with head up,breathing and panting.The rim without design is broad and has a flat surface.

Wu buffalo,refers to buffalo lives in area of Changjiang-Huaihe basin.The buffalo afraid of the hot weather and treat the moon as the sun,so it's laying on the ground and panting.

寿比南山铭镜　元代

直径8厘米，边厚0.6厘米，重51克

蚌埠市博物馆旧藏

　　圆形。桥钮。钮的两侧铸两竖行铭文，合铭为"寿比南山，福如东海"。其外环一周凸弦纹。卷缘。

Mirror with inscription of "Shou Bi Nan Shan"　Yuan Dynasty

Diameter:8cm,Thickness of rim:0.6cm,Weight:51gram

Collection of Bengbu Museum

　　The mirror is round in shape and has a bridge-shaped knob.Each side of the knob is adored with a vertical line of inscription, "Fu Ru Dong Hai"at the left side and "Shou Bi Nan Shan"at the right side.The major motif is surrounded with a band of raised string pattern.The rim is rolling.

仲明铭镜　元代

直径7厘米，边厚0.45厘米，重64克

蚌埠市博物馆旧藏

　　圆形。圆钮，钮顶平。钮的上下各铸一字铭，合读为"仲　　尊其瞻视"。卷缘。
明"。钮的左右两侧，各铸一竖行四字铭文，合读为"正其衣冠，

Mirror with inscription of "Zhong Ming"　Yuan Dynasty

Diameter:7cm,Thickness of rim:0.45cm,Weight:64gram

Collection of Bengbu Museum

　　The mirror is round in shape.It has a round knob with flat top. At the top and bottom sides are adored with two inscriptions "Zhong Ming", "Zhong"on the top and "Ming"at the bottom.Both right and left sides are decorated with two vertical lines of four inscriptions, "Zheng Qi Yi Guan"at the right side and "Zun Qi Zhan Shi"at the left side.The rim is rolling upward.

寿字铭仿汉带柄镜　元代

直径7.2厘米，执柄长8.1厘米，柄宽1.4厘米，边厚0.3厘米，重116克

蚌埠市博物馆旧藏

　　圆形，有柄。镜背纹饰是仿汉代昭明镜的纹饰。中间饰一浮雕　　糊，难以辨认，一周栉齿纹为廓。窄缘。
变形的"寿"字，其外饰内向八连弧纹，再外为铭文圈带，字体模

Imitation of Han Mirror with handle and inscription of "Shou"　Yuan Dynasty

Diameter:7.2cm,Length of handle:8.1cm,Width of handle:1.4cm,Thickness of rim:0.3cm,Weight:116gram

Collection of Bengbu Museum

　　The mirror is round in shape and has a handle.Patterns on the mirror back is the imitation of Mirror with inscription of Zhao Ming in Han Dynasty.The middle part is adored with a deformed "Shou" character in relief,outside the character are eight linked arcs inward. Then is a band of inscription with blurry font and hard to recognize.The major motif ends up with a band of fine-toothed pattern.The mirror has a narrow rim.

双鱼镜 明代

直径13.1厘米，边厚0.45厘米，重199克

蚌埠市博物馆旧藏

　　圆形。平顶圆钮。钮的两侧各饰一翘首张口、展鳍摆尾、作腾　　外置一周凸弦纹。窄缘。
跃状的鲤鱼纹，两鱼形态一致，头尾相接。两鱼相接处饰水草纹。

Mirror with design of double fish　Ming Dynasty

Diameter:13.1cm,Thickness of rim:0.45cm,Weight:199gram

Collection of Bengbu Museum

　　The mirror is round in shape and has a round knob with flat top. There are two carps,which are raising heads,opening mouths,spreading fins and swinging tails,at both sides of the knob.Both carps have the same shape and one's head connects to another carp's tail.The carps are spaced with two water weed pattern in vertical line.The major motif ends with a band of fine-toothed pattern.The mirror has a narrow rim.

双鱼镜　*明代*

直径14.3厘米，边厚0.55厘米，重283克

1980年临淮供销社征集

　　圆形。圆钮。钮的左右各饰一翘首张口、展鳍摆尾、作腾跃　　贵"，下方饰铭文"金玉满堂"。外置一周凸弦纹。窄缘。

状的鲤鱼纹，两鱼形态一致，头尾相接。钮的上方饰铭文"长命富

Mirror with design of double fish   Ming Dynasty

Diameter:14.3cm,Thickness of rim:0.55cm,Weight:283gram

Collected from Supply and Marketing Cooperatives in 1980

The mirror is round in shape and has a round knob.There are two carps,which are raising heads,opening mouths,spreading fins and swinging tails,at both sides of the knob.Both carps have the same shape and one's head connects to another carp's tail.At the top side of the knob is adored with four inscriptions of "Chang Ming Fu Gui"in vertical line,while "Jin Yu Man Tang" at the bottom.The major motif ends with a band of raised string pattern.The mirror has a narrow rim.

洪武二十二年铭云龙镜 明代

直径11厘米，边厚0.6厘米，重327克

1980年临淮供销社征集

　　圆形。山形钮。钮右侧一龙腾于云海之中，龙首在钮下，身躯蟠曲于上，前肢伸展，一后肢与龙尾缠绕，另一后肢仅露五爪。龙首前有云气缠绕。左侧一方框内有铭文"洪武二十二年正月日造"。素宽平缘。

Mirror with inscription of "Hong Wu Er Shi Er Nian"and design of cloud and dragon Ming Dynasty

Diameter:11cm,Thickness of rim:0.6cm,Weight:327gram

Collection of Bengbu Museum

The mirror is round in shape and has a mountain-shaped knob. At the right side of the knob is a dragon flying in the clouds with head hide under the knob,body curling on the knob,forelimbs stretching,one hind limb twisting with its tail,the other hind limb exposing five paws only.There are lots of clouds and steam before the dragon's head.At the left side of the knob is a rectangle with inscription of "Hong Wu Er Shi Er Nian Zheng Yue Ri Zao".The broad rim without design has a plat surface.

人物多宝镜　　明代

边长6.7厘米，边厚0.5厘米，重184克

1984年固镇出土

　　方形。银锭钮。钮两侧各饰一人，面向中心手持宝物；钮上置　框。窄缘。
一犀角；钮下依次饰盘肠、方胜和银锭。主纹饰外环一周凸起的方

Mirror with design of figures and treasures　　Ming Dynasty

Diameter:6.7cm,Thickness of rim:0.5cm,Weight:184gram

Unearthed at Guzhen in 1984

　　The mirror is in shape of square and has a silver-ingot-shaped knob.There are two persons,which are holding treasures,facing the center,at both sides of the knob.The top side of the knob is adored with a rhinoceros horn while the bottom are arranging with auspicious knot,intersecting lozenge and silver coin.Outside the major motif is a band of raised string pattern.The mirror has a narrow rim.

人物多宝镜　明代

直径7.4厘米，边厚0.1厘米，重56克

1980年临淮供销社征集

圆形，镜体极薄。银锭钮。纹饰由上至下分五个层次排列：最上方一展翅曲颈仙鹤，两侧各饰一对犀角；第二层中为方胜，两侧各有宝珠三粒；第三层即钮的两侧，各饰一银锭；第四层为二书卷；最下方正中一座聚宝盆，上盛仙果什物，两侧方胜与宝钱。中部外侧各一人，面向中心，手持宝物。

Mirror with design of figures and treasures　Ming Dynasty

Diameter:7.4cm,Thickness of rim:0.1cm,Weight:56gram

Collection of Bengbu Museum

The mirror is round in shape with a very thin body.It has a silver ingot shaped knob.The decoration on its back side is divided into five layers:at the top layer is a crane adored with a pair of rhinoceros horns on its both sides,which is stretching wings and bending neck;the second layer is intersecting lozenge with decoration of three treasure beads on both sides of the lozenge;the third layer are two silver ingots on both sides of the knob;the fourth layer are two book scroll.At the middle part of the bottom is a treasure basin with fruits and treasures inside,and decorations of intersecting lozenge and coins on both sides of the basin. Both outer sides of middle part is a person standing face the center and holding treasures.

仙阁四人多宝镜 明代

直径10.8厘米，边厚0.9厘米，重219克

蚌埠市博物馆旧藏

　　圆形。银锭钮。纹饰由上至下分三个层次排列：最上方中心一座二层仙阁，两侧为振翅高飞的仙鹤，鹤下分别饰有宝钱和花叶；钮上置一对犀牛角，两侧各二人，手持托盘，做行走状；钮下置一香炉，两侧为宝瓶，再外侧有方胜、宝钱、双犀角及书卷。窄缘。

Mirror with design of pavilion,four people and treasures Ming Dynasty

Diameter:10.8cm,Thickness of rim:0.9cm,Weight:219gram

Collection of Bengbu Museum

The mirror is round in shape and has a silver-ingot-shaped knob. The decoration on its back side is divided into three layers:at the top is a two-story pavilion and a pair of flying cranes on each side,coins and leaves below;on the knob is adored with a pair of rhinoceros horns and two people on each side of the knob,moving and holding tray;under the knob is a incense burner with vase on both sides,and intersecting lozenge,coins,two rhinoceros horns and book scroll.The mirror has a narrow rim.

长命富贵铭镜　明代

直径13厘米，边厚0.6厘米，重450克

蚌埠市博物馆旧藏

　　圆形。圆钮，钮顶平。钮的上下左右各铸一字铭，合读为"长命富贵"，其中"长"与"富"字之间长方形框内有一竖行铭文，字体漫漶。其外环一周凸弦纹，窄缘。

Mirror with inscription of "Chang Ming Fu Gui"　Ming Dynasty

Diameter:13cm,Thickness of rim:0.6cm,Weight:450gram

Collection of Bengbu Museum

　　The mirror is round in shape.It has a round knob with a flat top.At the four sides of the knob are adored with four inscriptions of "Chang Ming Fu Gui" which arranged in succession.Among that there is a rectangle with a vertical line of inscription inside between "Chang" and "Fu".The font is blurry and hard to recognize.The major motif is ends with a band of raised string pattern.The mirror has a narrow rim.

长命富贵铭镜 明代

直径21.6厘米，边厚0.7厘米，重1750克

蚌埠市博物馆旧藏

　　圆形。圆钮，仿汉龙虎钮座。钮外上下左右各铸一字铭，合读为"长命富贵"。各字间饰浮雕人物，四人形态各异，栩栩如生，每人各配一小纹饰，有花卉、草叶、蜂蝶等。其外环一周凸弦纹。窄缘。

Mirror with inscription of "Chang Ming Fu Gui" Ming Dynasty

Diameter:21.6cm,Thickness of rim:0.7cm,Weight:1750gram

Collection of Bengbu Museum

　　The mirror is round in shape.It has a round knob on a base with design of dragon and tiger which imitate Han Dynasty style.At the four sides of the knob are adored with four inscriptions of "Chang Ming Fu Gui" which arranged in succession.The characters are spaced with four vivid person in relief with different shapes,each person decorated with a small pattern like flower,leaf,butterfly and so on.A band of raised string pattern surrounds the major motif.The mirror has a narrow rim.

五子登科铭镜　明代
直径16.5厘米，边厚0.75厘米，重700克
蚌埠市博物馆旧藏

　　圆形。圆钮，钮顶平。钮外上下左右各有一凸起的方框，框内各铸一楷书字铭，合读为"五子登科"。各字间饰一浮雕人物，手持托盘，做行走状。其外环一周凸弦纹，窄缘。

　　《宋史·窦仪传》记载：五代后晋时期，窦禹钧的五个儿子相继及第，称"五子登科"。

Mirror with inscription of "Wu Zi Deng Ke" Ming Dynasty

Diameter:16.5cm,Thickness of rim:0.75cm,Weight:700gram

Collection of Bengbu Museum

The mirror is round in shape and has a round knob with a flat top. At the four sides of the knob are four raised square with characters of "Wu Zi Deng Ke" arranged in succession and carved in standard script. The characters are spaced with four moving persons holding tray in relief.Outside the major motif is a band of raised string pattern.The mirror has a narrow rim.

According to the record in *Dou Yi Zhuan of Song History*,in the Five Dynasties and Ten Kingdoms,the five sons of Dou Yujun succeeded in the civil examinations and became high officials,hence the name of "Wu Zi Deng Ke".

五子登科铭镜 明代

直径22厘米，边厚0.9厘米，重1150克

蚌埠市博物馆旧藏

　　圆形。圆钮，钮顶平。钮外饰一周瑞兽纹。其外四方各置一方　　卉等图案。窄缘。
框，框内铭文合读为"五子登科"。字与字之间饰有童子持宝及花

Mirror with inscription of "Wu Zi Deng Ke" Ming Dynasty

Diameter:22cm,Thickness of rim:0.9cm,Weight:1150gram

Collection of Bengbu Museum

　　The mirror is round in shape. It has a round knob with a flat top. Outside the knob is a band of auspicious beast pattern. At the four sides of the knob are four squares with inscription of "Wu Zi Deng Ke". The characters are spaced with boys holding treasures and flowers. The mirror has a narrow rim.

福寿双全五子登科双铭镜 明代

直径15.2厘米，边厚0.8厘米，重298克

蚌埠市博物馆旧藏

　　圆形。圆钮。钮外上下左右各有一个凸起的大方框，框内各铸一字铭，合读为"福寿双全"，各字又间饰一小方框，框内各铸一字，合读为"五子登科"。"福"与"五"字之间置一圆枚，其外环一周凸弦纹。窄缘。

Mirror with double inscriptions of "Fu Shou Shuang Quan"and"Wu Zi Deng Ke" Ming Dynasty

Diameter:15.2cm,Thickness of rim:0.8cm,Weight:298gram

Collection of Bengbu Museum

　　The mirror is round in shape and has a round knob.At the four sides of the knob are four raised square with inscriptions of "Fu Shou Shuang Quan".The characters are spaced with four small squares with characters of "Wu Zi Deng Ke".Between the character Fu and Wu is a round seal with an unclear inscription which is hard to recognize. Outside the major motif is a band of raised string pattern.The mirror has a narrow rim.

三元及第铭镜 明代

直径10.2厘米，边厚0.3厘米，重275克
蚌埠市博物馆旧藏

　　圆形。圆钮，钮顶平。钮外上下左右各有一凸起的方框，框内各铸一楷书字铭，合读为"三元及第"。其外环一周凸弦纹，窄缘。

　　科举制度称乡试、会试、殿试的第一名为解元、会元、状元，合称"三元"。三元及第表示在科举考试中，乡试、会试、殿试都取得第一名。历史上获此殊荣的仅有15人，可谓凤毛麟角。

Mirror with inscription of "San Yuan Ji Di"　Ming Dynasty

Diameter:10.2cm, Thickness of rim:0.3cm, Weight:275gram
Collection of Bengbu Museum

　　The mirror is round in shape.It has a round knob with a flat knob. At the four sides of the knob are four raised squares with characters of "San Yuan Ji Di" arranged in succession and carved in standard script. Outside the characters is a band of raised string pattern.The mirror has a narrow rim.

　　"San Yan" refers to the extremely man who was the first on the pass lists of each of three levels of civil service recruitment examinations, including Provincial Examination,Metropolitan Examination and Palace Examinations.There were only 15 men who got "San Yan Ji Di" in the history.

状元及第铭镜 明代

直径14.2厘米，边厚0.3厘米，重548克

蚌埠市博物馆旧藏

圆形。圆钮。钮外上下左右各有一凸起的方框，框内各铸一楷书字铭，合读为"状元及第"。其外环一周凸弦纹，窄缘。

Mirror with inscription of "Zhuang Yuan Ji Di" Ming Dynasty

Diameter:14.2cm,Thickness of rim:0.3cm,Weight:548gram

Collection of Bengbu Museum

The mirror is round in shape and has a round knob.At the four sides of the knob are four raised squares with inscriptions of "Zhuang Yuan Ji Di" which arranged in succession and carved in standard script. Outside the characters is a band of raised string pattern.The mirror has a narrow rim.

百寿团圆铭镜　明代

直径31.5厘米，边厚2厘米，重2950克

蚌埠市博物馆旧藏

　　圆形。圆钮，钮外饰一周瑞兽纹。其外四方各置一方框，框　　瓶、八宝等图案。
内铭"百寿团圆"四字，每字之间饰有童子持宝及祥云、花篮、花

Mirror with inscription of "Bai Shou Tuan Yuan"　Ming Dynasty

Diameter:31.5cm,Thickness of rim:2cm,Weight:2950gram

Collection of Bengbu Museum

　　The mirror is round in shape and has a round knob.Outside the knob is a band of auspicious beast pattern.At the four sides of the knob are four squares with characters of "Bai Shou Tuan Yuan" arranged in succession.The characters are spaced with designs of boys holding treasures,auspicious clouds,blanket with flowers,vase,eight treasures and so on.

寿山福海铭镜 明代

直径12.3厘米，边厚0.4厘米，重221克

蚌埠市博物馆旧藏

　　圆形。圆钮。钮外上下左右各有一凸起的方框，框内各铸一楷书字铭，合读为"寿山福海"，在"海"与"寿"字之间长方形框为有两竖行铭文"李盛州真青铜"。其外环一周凸弦纹。窄缘。

Mirror with inscription of "Shou Shan Fu Hai" Ming Dynasty

Diameter:12.3cm,Thickness of rim:0.4cm,Weight:221gram

Collection of Bengbu Museum

　　The mirror is round in shape and has a round knob.At the four sides of the knob are four raised squares with characters of "Shou Shan Fu Hai" arranged in succession and carved in standard script.There is a rectangle between characters of "Shou" and "Hai",with inscriptions of "Li Sheng Zhou Zhen Qing Tong" in two vertical lines.A band of raised string pattern surrounds them.The mirror has a narrow rim.

喜生贵子铭镜　明代

直径31厘米，边厚1.9厘米，重4085克

蚌埠市博物馆旧藏

　　圆形。圆钮，钮外饰一周瑞兽纹。钮外置四方框，框内各铸一字，合读为"喜生贵子"。每字之间饰有童子持宝及祥云、花篮、花瓶、八宝等图案。此镜尺寸较大，制作精美，纹饰丰富，为此类镜中的上乘之作。

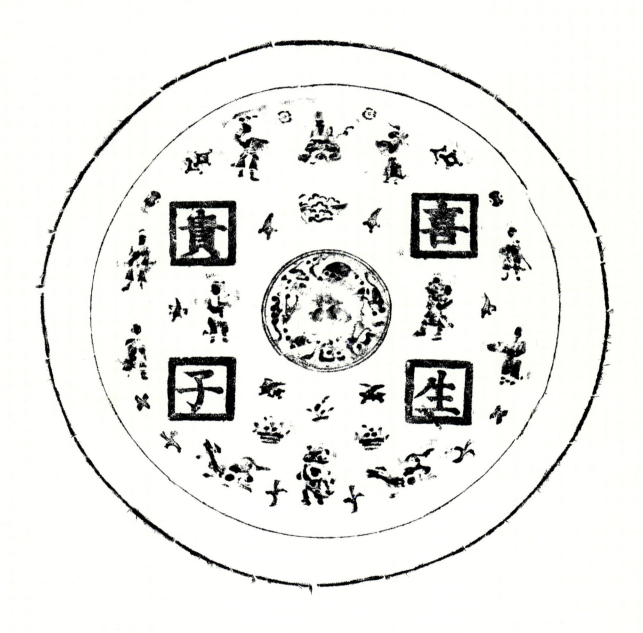

Mirror with inscription of "Xi Sheng Gui Zi" Ming Dynasty

Diameter:31cm,Thickness of rim:1.9cm,Weight:4085gram

Collection of Bengbu Museum

The mirror is round in shape and has a round knob.Outside the knob is a band of auspicious beast pattern.Outside the pattern are four squares with characters of "Xi Sheng Gui Zi" .Each character is spaced with decorations of boys holding treasures,auspicious clouds,blanket with flowers,vase,eight treasures and so on.The mirror has a big size with delicate mold and exquisite designs,is the treasure of the bronze mirror.

仲明铭镜　明代

直径8.3厘米，边厚0.5厘米，重103克

蚌埠市博物馆旧藏

　　圆形。圆钮。钮的上下各铸一字铭，合铭为"仲明"。素宽缘。

Mirror with inscription of "Zhong Ming"　Ming Dynasty

Diameter:8.3cm,Thickness of rim:0.5cm,Weight:103gram

Collection of Bengbu Museum

　　The mirror is round in shape and has a round knob.Both the top and bottom sides of the knob is adored with a inscription, "Zhong" at the top and "Ming" at the bottom.The rim without design is broad.

为善最乐铭镜　明代
直径6.8厘米，边厚0.25厘米，重48克
蚌埠市博物馆旧藏

　　圆形。银锭钮。钮的左右两侧各铸两个楷书字铭，合读为"为善最乐"。其外环一周凸弦纹。窄缘。

　　"为善最乐"一词最早出自《后汉书·东平宪王苍传》："日者问东平王，处家何等最乐？王言为善最乐。"此后，成为后人常用的劝世格言。

Mirror with inscription of "Wei Shan Zui Le"　Ming Dynasty
Diameter:6.8cm,Thickness of rim:0.25cm,Weight:48gram
Collection of Bengbu Museum

　　The mirror is round in shape and has a silver-ingot-shaped knob. Both sides of the knob are adored with two inscriptions which carved in standard script, "Wei Shan" at the right side and "Zui Le" at the left side.Outside the characters is a band of raised string pattern.The mirror has a narrow rim.

　　The words came from *Dong Ping Xian Wang Cang Zhuan of Hou Han Shu* for the first time.Since then,it became a maxim when people used for persuading.

湖州孙家铭镜　明代

直径8.2厘米，边厚0.3厘米，重56.5克

蚌埠市博物馆旧藏

　　圆形。银锭钮。钮的左右两侧，各置一圭形框，框内各铸四字铭文"湖州孙家，青鸾宝鉴"。其外环一周凸弦纹。卷缘。

Mirror with inscription of "Hu Zhou Sun Jia"　Ming Dynasty

Diameter:8.2cm,Thickness of rim:0.3cm,Weight:56.5gram

Collection of Bengbu Museum

　　The mirror is round in shape and has a silver-ingot-shaped knob. Both the right and left sides of the knob are adored with a Gui-shaped frame with four inscriptions, "Hu Zhou Sun Jia" at the right side while "Qing Luan Bao Jian" at the left side. A band of raised pattern surrounds the major motif. The rim is rolling.

湖州薛怀泉造铭素镜　明代

直径13.7厘米，边厚0.45厘米，重605克
蚌埠市博物馆旧藏

　　圆形。柱状钮，钮顶平。钮顶铸阳文楷书六字铭文，合读为
"湖州薛怀泉造"，镜背通体素面无纹饰。钮顶铸字，为明代首创。

Mirror with inscription of "Hu Zhou Xue Huai Quan Zao"　Ming Dynasty

Diameter:13.7cm,Thickness of rim:0.45cm,Weight:605gram
Collection of Bengbu Museum

　　The mirror is round in shape.It has a pillar-shaped knob with a flat top.On the top of the knob are six raised inscriptions of "Hu Zhou Xue Huai Quan Zao" carved in standard script.Its back side showing no design.

　　Characters carved on knob top is created in Ming Dynasty for the first time.

弦纹镜 明代
直径13.5厘米，边厚1.1厘米，重520克
1978年本市征集

　　圆形。圆钮，钮顶平。钮外环一周高圈凸弦纹。双重素窄边。

Mirror with convex string design Ming Dynasty
Diameter:13.5cm,Thickness of rim:1.1cm,Weight:520gram
Collected from Bengbu City in 1978

　　The mirror is round in shape.It has a round knob with a flat top. Outside the knob is a band of high raised convex string pattern.Both two rims showing no design have a narrow edge.

李字铭仿汉禽兽纹简化博局镜 明代
直径10.5厘米，边厚0.45厘米，重218克
蚌埠市博物馆旧藏

　　圆形。圆钮，圆钮座，钮顶平。座外围双线方框一周。其外
置四乳钉和"T"、"L"形简化博局纹，乳钉纹和博局纹的空白处
填饰八只禽兽，有白虎、青龙、禽兽和禽鸟等，钮的外侧"T"、

"L"博局纹之上有一圆形阳文"李"字印记。宽缘，缘上饰一周
变形蟠虺纹。

Imitation of Han Mirror with inscription of "Li"and design of four animals and simple gambling Ming Dynasty
Diameter:10.5cm,Thickness of rim:0.45cm,Weight:218gram
Collection of Bengbu Museum

　　The mirror is round in shape.It has a round knob with a flat top
on a round base.Outside the base is a square formed by double lines.
Outside the square are four nipples and TL-shaped simple gambling
design which spaced with eight beasts like White Tiger,Green

Dragon,Beasts,Birds and so on.There is a round raised character "Li"
on ⊓.L-shaped gambling design at the left side of the knob.On the broad
rim is a band of deformed serpent design.

祁怀园造铭仿汉四神博局镜 明代

直径19.3厘米，边厚0.8厘米，重1550克
蚌埠市博物馆旧藏

圆形。圆钮，钮顶平，柿蒂纹钮座。座外围一周双线凹面方框，钮座与方框间饰十二地支铭文和十二个圆座小乳钉。方框外饰八枚圆座乳钉和"T、L、V"博局纹。乳钉纹和博局纹将镜背分成四方八区，空白处填饰青龙、白虎、朱雀、玄武四神，各据一方，每神配一只禽兽作装饰，隔"V"纹相对而立。钮的左右两侧各置一长方形方框，框内铸"祁怀园造"四字铭文。其外一周铭文圈带："王氏昭竟四夷服，多贺新家人民息，官位□□天下复，风雨□节五□□，长保二□子孙力，传告后世乐毋极。"宽缘，缘上饰锯齿纹和云气纹各一周。

Imitation of Han Mirror with inscription of "Qi Huai Yuan Zao"and design of four deities and gambling Ming Dynasty

Diameter:19.3cm,Thickness of rim:0.8cm,Weight:1550gram

Collected from Bengbu City in 1978

The mirror is round in shape.It has a round knob with a flat top on a base with kaki calyx design.Outside the base is a concave surface square formed by double lines.Twelve small nipples with round base arranged in a square adored between the base and the concave surface square and is spaced with twelve Earthly Branches.Outside the concave surface square are eight nipples with round base and T.L.V.-shaped gambling design which divided the mirror back into four zones.The major motif is decorated with Green Dragon,White Tiger,Scarlet Bird and Somber Warrior.Each deity is adored with a beast at the corner of the square and standing face to face by the V design.Both sides of the knob is a rectangle with inscription of "Qi Huai Yuan Zao".Outside the major motif is a band of inscription "Wang Shi Zhao Jing Si Yi Fu,Duo He Xin Jia Ren Min Xi,Guan Wei□□Tian Xia Fu,Feng Yu□Jie Wu□□,Chang Bao Er□Zi Sun Li,Chuan Gao Hou Shi Le Wu Ji".On the broad rim are a band of saw design and a band of cloud design.

双喜五蝠纹带柄镜　*清代*

直径16.6厘米，执柄残长1.6厘米，柄宽2.2厘米，边厚0.2厘米，重251克

蚌埠市博物馆旧藏

　　圆形。带柄，柄残。镜中心饰双喜字，在喜字外围一凸面圈带，其外饰有五个展翅飞翔的蝙蝠。在柄端的两蝙蝠之间有铭文四字"毛义泰造"。窄缘。

双喜镜为清代创新的流行镜类。五蝠谐音五福，取福意。五福，清代多指福、禄、寿、喜、财，是一种吉祥纹饰。

Mirror with handle and design of double "xi" and five bats   Qing Dynasty

Diameter:16.6cm,Incomplete length of handle:1.6cm,Width of handle:2.2cm,Thickness of rim:0.2cm,Weight:251gram

Collection of Bengbu Museum

The mirror is round in shape.It has an incomplete handle.The middle part is decorated with double "Xi" which surrounded by a band of raised surface pattern.Outside the band are five bats,spreading wings and flying.Between the two bats which nearby the top of handle is adored with four inscription of "Mao Yi Tai Zao".The mirror has a narrow rim.

Mirror with double Xi was created and popular in Qing Dynasty. The five bats have the same pronunciation with five fu in Chinese,is a kind of auspicious pattern,which means blessing,prosperity,long life,happiness and wealth in Qing Dynasty.

苕溪薛惠公造铭文镜　清代

边长10厘米，重148克
蚌埠市博物馆旧藏

方形，无钮。镜背铸16字楷书铭文，"方正而明，万里无尘。水天一色，犀照群伦"。左下角铸篆书"苕溪"圆形章和"薛惠公造"方形章各一枚。素宽平缘。

薛惠公，名晋候，字惠公，号苕溪，清乾隆时人，以铸镜素有佳名。

Mirror with inscription of "Shao Xi Xue Hui Gong Zao"　Qing Dynasty

Length of side:10cm,Thickness of rim:0.2cm,Weight:148gram
Collection of Bengbu Museum

The mirror is in shape of square.It has no knob and lack of a corner.On the back of mirror,there are sixteen regular words "Fang Zheng Er Mig,Wan Li Wu Chen,Shui Tian Yi Se,Xi Zhao Qun Lun".On the left bottom, there are round badge with two seal characters "Shao Xi" and square badge with "Xue Hui Gong Zao".Xuehui Gong's name is Jinhou,also called Tiaoxi.He was a man of Qianlong era,and famous for coining mirror.

后 记 POSTSCRIPT

后 记

蚌埠博物馆始建于1974年，到今天，已经走过了四十个年头。建馆之初，为了丰富馆藏文物，老一辈文物工作者从市物资回收公司拣选一大批青铜器，其中不乏历代铜镜。随着文物事业的蓬勃发展，通过考古发掘、征集、接受捐赠、公安部门移交等途径，馆藏铜镜的种类和数量不断攀升，现藏品已达500余面，成为馆藏青铜器类别的一个大项。将这些铜镜整理和研究很有必要，同时也是萦绕在我馆文物工作者心头多年的夙愿。

本书铜镜筛选时兼顾铜镜的时代性及珍贵性，择优选取，尽可能地将馆藏最精品的铜镜提供给读者；编排时以"时代为主线、类别为辅线"的原则，来向读者展示本馆藏镜，同时辅以拓片，力求将每面铜镜所包含的历史信息全面地传达给读者。

《蚌埠市博物馆藏镜集萃》是我馆第一部专题性的文物图录著作，在书籍编写过程中遇到各种新问题，全馆同志积极查找相关资料，请教兄弟单位，共同解决难题，在馆内形成了良好的学习氛围，业务水平也得到了提高。当然，作为地市级博物馆，受藏品体系的制约，想要出版一本完全反映历代铜镜面貌的作品，实难为之。加之我们的专业素养和认知水平有限，本书中谬误之处，还望斧正。

《蚌埠市博物馆藏镜集萃》的出版，适逢新馆开馆之际，愿谨以此书为新馆开放的喜庆氛围增添一抹亮色。本书得到了蚌埠市文化广电新闻出版局、蚌埠市财政局的大力支持。淮南市博物馆馆长沈汗青先生，在工作十分繁忙的情况下，认真对书稿予以审校。萧县博物馆周水利先生、王侠女士、苏慧芳女士、孙伟先生、张影女士、程桂芝女士为拓片制作付出了艰苦的努力。徐大立先生承担了统稿工作。王维凤先生承担了铜镜拍摄工作。陈新宇、王元宏、尤薇娜、秦梦士等同志，不辞辛苦承担了书稿全部文字的录入工作和编务工作。尤薇娜同志为本书提供了英文翻译。在此向成书过程中付出辛勤努力的同仁，致以由衷的感谢！

编者

2014年7月26日

Postscript

It has been forty years since the founding of Bengbu Museum from 1974. At the beginning, the last generation of workers in our museum chose and picked a large number of bronze ware from the material recycling companies which including ancient bronze mirrors through the dynasties, in order to enrich the cultural relics there. As the vigorous development of cultural and museum industry, the Bengbu Museum has built up a fine collection of bronze mirror in both species and quantity by means of archaeological excavating, collecting, donating, transferring from public security bureaus. The number has been reached more than 500 which occupy a large major in collection category of bronze ware. It is vital to classify and conduct study these bronze mirrors, which linger on our minds for many years.

Due to the purpose of reflecting the continuity of the times and presenting the value, the bronze mirrors' list in the book were selected from the best of the collection. We will show the most exquisite mirrors to readers as far as possible. The bronze mirrors' list in the book, takes "Time is the main line while category is the auxiliary one" as a principle to lay out. At the same time, with the supplement of rubbing, we strive to transmit the historic information to the readers completely.

The Competitive Collection of Bronze Mirrors at Bengbu Museum is the first special catalogue monograph on cultural relics. Editing this book is a process of enhancing professional knowledge for all staffs of the Bengbu Museum. We have met many new problems during the work. There is a good study atmosphere in our museum, with each staff looking for references, asking for help from other units and solving problems together. Certainly, based on the collection of a city-level museum, it is not easy, even difficult, to edit and public a specialized book, which reflects the mirrors through the ages. Due to our limited professional knowledge and cognitive level, the book may has many deficiencies. We sincerely hope and welcome the readers point them out so that they can be corrected.

The publication of *Sdected Collection of Bronze Mirrors at Bengbu Museum* coincides with the occasion of our new museum opening up, so we sincerely hope this book can bring and add a bright color for the festive mood. The publication work has gained the enormous support from the Culture, Radio, Television, Press and Publication Bureau of Bengbu City and the Finance Bureau of Bengbu City. Mr. Shen Hanqing, curator of the Huainan Museum, carefully revised this book under the condition of his busy work. Mr. Zhou Shuili, Ms. Wang Xia, Ms. Su Huifang, Mr. Sun Wei, Ms. Zhang Wei, Ms. Zhang Ying and Ms. Cheng Guizhi, the experts from the Xiaoxian Museum, made their hard efforts for rubbing. Mr. Wang Weifeng took photos for this book. Chen Xinyu, Wang Yuanhong, You Weina and Qin Mengshi assumed all the words inputting and editing work. You Weina took work on translating the book into English. The final contributor is Ms. Xu Dali. Give our hearty thanks to these hard-working members!

Compiler
July 26, 2014

责任编辑：李　东

责任印制：张　丽

图书在版编目（ＣＩＰ）数据

　蚌埠市博物馆铜镜集萃 ／ 蚌埠市博物馆编著． —— 北京 ：文物出版社，2014.10
　ISBN 978-7-5010-4087-2

　Ⅰ．①蚌⋯ Ⅱ．①蚌⋯ Ⅲ．①古镜－铜器（考古）－鉴赏－蚌埠市 Ⅳ．①K875.22

　中国版本图书馆CIP数据核字(2014)第212098号

蚌埠市博物馆铜镜集萃

编　　者	蚌埠市博物馆	
出版发行	文物出版社	
社　　址	北京市东直门内北小街2号楼	
网　　址	www.wenwu.com	
邮　　箱	web@wenwu.com	
制版印刷	北京图文天地制版印刷有限公司	
经　　销	新华书店	
开　　本	889×1194　1/16	
印　　张	14.25	
版　　次	2014年10月第1版	
印　　次	2014年10月第1次印刷	
书　　号	ISBN 978-7-5010-4087-2	
定　　价	280.00元	